You Don't Have to Love Yourself

Ditch Self-Loathing, Heal Complex Trauma, and Find Peace in Self-Neutrality

Dr. Heidi Green

YOU DON'T HAVE TO LOVE YOURSELF

Published by
Bridge City Books, an imprint of PESI Publishing, Inc.
3839 White Ave
Eau Claire, WI 54703

Cover and interior design by Abby Isackson
Editing by Roseanne Cheng

ISBN 9781962305495 (print)
ISBN 9781962305501 (ePUB)
ISBN 9781962305518 (ePDF)

Printed in Canada.

This book is dedicated to every trauma survivor who has allowed me to be a part of their healing journey.

Table of Contents

INTRODUCTION

What Is Self-Neutrality?

When I first heard the term *self-neutrality*, I must admit I was a little confused. Was this concept suggesting people should have no feelings about themselves? As a therapist who has spent years encouraging my clients to seek self-love, I didn't understand where self-neutrality could fit into the world of mental health.

Perhaps you heard the term *self-neutrality* for the first time when you picked up this book. It might have spoken to you because you have felt uneasy or overwhelmed by the "self-love" movement on social media and in recent pop culture. When I think of self-neutrality as a healthy alternative to self-loathing, it makes much more sense. If you have ever balked at the concept of self-love, thinking, "I will never love myself. I don't even know what that means," I wrote this book just for you.

So, what is self-neutrality? Simply put, **self-neutrality is the ability to see yourself objectively, with unemotional and nonjudgmental curiosity and observation.** Self-neutrality turns self-statements like "I'm such an idiot" into "I made a mistake, and I feel upset with myself right now." Through the lens of self-neutrality, "My body is gross" becomes "My body is an acceptable human body, just like every other human body."

Think about all the emotions that come up when you're feeling down about yourself: the rage, the sadness, the fear of the unknown. Self-neutrality removes the emotion and judgment from your experience so you can acknowledge the facts and accept reality without making life's painful moments worse. This can be difficult to put into practice because so many of us have been trained to be critical and hateful toward ourselves.

As a psychologist who specializes in treating complex trauma, I have witnessed the angst in my clients' eyes time and again as they struggle with the idea that they could ever love themselves. Many survivors of childhood trauma enter therapy because they are full of self-loathing and can't bear the internalized pain anymore. Complex trauma often creates self-loathing because when children aren't adequately loved by their caregivers, it can feel impossible to love themselves in adulthood.

Think of complex trauma as a series of interpersonal traumas occurring throughout a child's life. A child can't grow to have a positive self-image if the adults in their world don't treat them like they are a lovable, valuable, worthy person. In fact, a child who is not given adequate positive affirmation will begin to see themselves as unlovable and unworthy. They will believe something is wrong with them, and that will likely carry into adulthood.

When an adult has been disliking themselves since childhood, it can be difficult to see themselves as lovable because they can't remember a time when they felt truly loved. Healthy adults can look back on their young selves and feel fondness for the child they once were. They still feel connected to that little person, like their younger self is still a part of them. We often refer to that young part that still lives in us as our "inner child."

As a trauma therapist, I've listened to so many clients describe hating their inner child. They see their young self as the cause of many of their current problems. They believe if they hadn't been so defective as a young person, they would have been worthy of love in childhood and could have grown into a worthy, lovable adult.

These clients hate the idea of sinking into their bodies. They can't meditate or practice mindfulness without having a panic attack or a flashback of a painful time in their past. Their bodies feel dirty, damaged, and unsafe. They have a never-ending monologue of self-condemnation running through their minds all day, every day.

If this sounds familiar, you may also feel incredibly unseen when you repeatedly read on the internet that you "just need to start practicing self-love" to heal and be happy. For the complex trauma survivor, nothing could feel further out of reach. I get it.

For those of you already familiar with my work, you might be thinking, "Didn't you already write an entire book on how to love yourself?" The answer is yes, I did. *The Path to Self-Love & World Domination* is a great book for people with a history of trauma who believe they can love themselves and who want to find a path to self-love by resolving their unhealed wounds. It's the right book for some, but it's not a book for everyone.

In contrast, this book is intended to help you cultivate a sense of neutrality toward the younger versions of yourself so you can ultimately build neutrality toward your present-day self. It will help you see how all your trauma responses were adaptive. Any other child in your situation would likely have responded in a similar way. I want to show you that what happened to you in childhood may have been terrible, but it wasn't because you were terrible. You were simply a child with limited resources, no power, and not enough cognitive development or life experience to have any idea how to handle what was going on.

It might sound counterintuitive to all the memes you see on Instagram, but in this book we are going to take self-love off the table. Instead, we are going to make a space where it's safe to explore the origins of self-hatred. We will dismantle those beliefs slowly and tenderly through challenging but attainable goals. In the first few chapters, we'll talk about how trauma has impacted your view of yourself. Then, we'll move into debunking some of the myths about self-love. Finally, we'll dive deep into the concept of self-neutrality and explore how you can implement it in your own life.

I don't want to pretend that this book is going to magically heal you. I need you to know that it's okay if you never feel fully healed. Many survivors, myself included, will always struggle with some aftereffects of trauma, no matter how much self-neutrality they practice. It's just like when a person lives through a major physical injury: scars and ongoing pain or limitations may still exist after the healing work is done.

There is nothing wrong with you if you can never enjoy meditating, never completely banish negative self-talk, or never feel full of self-love. You are simply a human being having a human experience, floating around with other humans who also struggle with pain, loss, insecurity, and fear. We are all out here trying to figure life out and none of us ever figure it out fully. In this book, you will seek self-neutrality by understanding your connections to others, rather than focusing on all the ways your trauma makes you feel different from and less than others.

You may be new to the concept of self-neutrality, but it just might be the answer you've been searching for. This book will take the pressure off "becoming your highest self," "achieving self-love," "embracing body positivity," or any of the other catchy quips on the internet that make you feel worse about yourself. Within these pages, I hope you will feel seen and understood. Looking at yourself with genuine empathy and compassion still might feel like an impossible ask, but please be open to exploring self-acceptance and self-neutrality. I will provide realistic options for releasing the grip your complex trauma holds over you.

The reality is you might never feel powerful and emboldened, at least not in the ways that social media might suggest you "should" be. Honestly, you might decide you don't need that. I will encourage you to discover what healing means to you from the lens of your unique life experiences. You can simply strive to feel more peaceful and safer in the mind and body you inhabit. Trauma occurs when bad things happen, and you have no power to control or stop it. Healing will occur when you acknowledge the many options you do have today and when you start using your power to choose options that are best for you.

Might this work lead you toward self-love someday? Maybe. But that doesn't need to be the end goal. Your peace will lie in deciding for yourself what resonates, what doesn't, where you want to focus your posttraumatic growth, and what's just not for you. Finding a state of neutrality toward your body, your past, your abusers, your inner child, your current thoughts, and even the world you live in today is where your deep healing can finally begin.

Ready to do this? Me too. Let's go.

CHAPTER 1

Make Peace with Your Personal Trauma History

No matter what your specific circumstances are, you picked up this book because you are looking to make peace with your personal trauma history. Trauma healing begins when you acknowledge how your life experiences impacted the adult you became. When you do that, you give yourself the power to change your life. When you view your struggles as the result of your experiences, you recognize that most of your unhelpful traits were learned and can thus be unlearned, which allows you to reclaim your power and ability to change yourself and your circumstances. Without this recognition, you may always believe that something is inherently wrong with you and that you're powerless to fix it.

Maybe the adults who raised you were truly terrible people. I've seen this many times. Maybe they weren't terrible people, but they were terrible at raising children. Perhaps they genuinely loved you and wanted to be good parents, but they were so limited in their parenting capabilities that their best was still far below the baseline to be a "good enough" parent.

Parents don't need to be perfect to raise healthy children. Thank goodness that there is a lot of room for error. But there are certain criteria that can identify if a caregiver is "good enough" to ensure their child grows into a healthy adult. For example, if your parents didn't ensure you felt safe, loved, and supported throughout your childhood, even if they "did their best," it may not have been good enough to meet your fundamental childhood needs and allow you to become a confident, healthy, self-loving adult.

Whatever the situation in your home growing up, you were certainly raised by imperfect people. We all have weaknesses. We all make mistakes. Good, loving parents do unhelpful things in their parenting that hurt their kids and distort their self-image and worldview. It's incredibly common, and it doesn't mean your parents were bad people or bad parents. It doesn't mean you have to be angry at them forever, confront them, or cut them out of your life. It just means the people who raised you were human. They were likely struggling with their own unresolved trauma or untreated mental health disorders, and their shortcomings had a negative impact on you. Your human shortcomings affect the people in your life too. It's totally normal and not something to be ashamed of. We are only human, and we're all fumbling through life trying to do our best.

However it came to be, you are now a person who has unresolved emotional wounding. That wounding is the reason you feel so terrible about yourself. Whatever story you have been telling yourself about how awful you are *is a lie*. You are not the exception. It doesn't matter that I don't know you or your story. I don't need to know all the details you think make you different. I'll tell you why.

I've spent countless hours in therapy sessions, holding space for people who, just like you, had a story about why they were truly more unworthy and unlovable than anyone else in the world. It didn't matter what their story was. They all felt the same. I'm an expert in human psychology, human behavior, and the impact of complex trauma on human psychology and behavior. As I will talk about throughout this book, we all think our stories are different, but we're incredibly similar. We all think we're the exception to humanity. No matter how different our trauma experiences were, we all end up feeling the same. Our complex traumas make us feel like rotten, disgusting, human trash bags. And we are all *wrong* about ourselves.

That's why I'm starting this book with my story. You came to me in your time of need, and change takes time and trust. Trust is a two-way street, so I am going to trust you now with my trauma story. I will share my deeply personal experiences with you because I want you to know that I get it. I know how much courage it takes to trust yourself and to trust this process.

I'm not a psychologist sitting on my armchair like it's a throne, professing to be perfect or all-knowing. I've screwed up more times than I will ever recount. In fact, I've screwed things up so monumentally, so many times, that I've finally gotten pretty good at repairing with others and myself when I make a mess of things. I still make a lot of mistakes. I sometimes overreact when I get triggered. I can be mean when I go into self-protection mode. Sometimes I'm selfish and unreasonable, even though I don't want to be. Occasionally, I fall back into a state of temporary self-loathing. I hurt people I love, and they hurt me. That's the reality of life.

Like you, I am an adult survivor of childhood trauma and abuse. I had to reconcile the trauma inflicted on me by parents who failed me, and honestly, it's an ongoing process. I have also been the parent who failed my children even though I was "doing my best."

My best wasn't always good enough and it was easy to tell myself it was because I was a shitty, worthless, horrible person and mother. But that wasn't true. Moreover, shaming myself wasn't helpful to the people who needed me.

My self-hatred caused nothing but problems in my life, and when I finally began to accept the problem wasn't me, but what *happened* to me, everything about my life started to get a little brighter.

I grew up with an alcoholic mother and an abusive stepfather. (My father, as you'll learn shortly, was not around very much.) My mom was very loving but extremely childlike, and she did not protect me from her husband's violence. I held the secret of my abuse until I became pregnant at fifteen years old. I could no longer protect my stepfather's disgusting secret once I knew I was bringing my own innocent child into the world. Like it often does, speaking the truth out loud created so many problems for me. In some ways, I continue to live with these repercussions. However, I once heard another author say something like "If people wanted you to write nice things about them, they should have treated you better." So, I may as well not stop telling the truth now.

My mom drank heavily to numb the pain of her husband's abuse and effectively left me to fend for myself. It was so confusing to grow up in a home where I had a caring parent who was attentive to me in many ways but who also permitted abuse to be perpetrated upon me. As Mom numbed it all out with alcohol, I had to endure the abuse alone, as a child, sober, and in desperate need of protection.

My stepfather abused me in every way a man can abuse a child, but by far the most frequent and damaging was the barrage of emotional abuse that went on in our home virtually every day.

I wonder now if he had an undiagnosed psychological condition because he was quite fun, spontaneous, and funny some days. But mostly, he was gruff, moody, and distant. I was happy for any day that didn't involve objects being thrown across the room, him screaming and raging into my face so close that he spat on me, watching my mother sob and beg him to stop as he called her a "fucking idiot" or a "piece-of-shit moron," hiding in my bedroom (if I could), or enduring the incredibly foul things he said to me about me.

My stepfather loved the power trip of controlling and dominating the females in his home. I was such a smart, intuitive child that I often saw right through his unsophisticated mind games. I always knew he was unhinged, and the crazy (if not evil) things he said and did were completely wrong. I was stubborn and didn't want to let him "win" the games he forced us to play. Being so stubborn set me up for more intense abuse (so for all you childhood trauma survivors who kick yourselves for not "doing something" or "speaking up," you were probably smart to protect yourselves from potentially more abuse). My mom was a nurse who worked nights, so the worst of the abuse happened on the evenings she wasn't home. I was terrified every time I knew I would be alone with him at night.

One night, my stepfather took me up to our rooftop deck and laid into me about how much my parents didn't want me. "They fight over who has to take care of you because neither of them wants you." I knew for certain he was lying, and I decided the only way to keep him from "winning" was for me to endure his tirade without crying. I knew all he wanted was to break me, and even at my tender elementary-school age, I just didn't want to be broken.

This meant I stared him in the eyes as he escalated his abuse. "You are the spawn of Satan," he said at one point. Even though he sounded ridiculous to me, I was still just a little girl. I don't know how long I stayed up on that roof letting him verbally attack me. It felt like over an hour, but it might have been ten minutes. Childhood memories are spotty in that way, so I'll never really know.

Eventually, I became exhausted, and all I wanted was to go back inside and get the hell away from him, so I gave myself permission to cry. I sobbed the way I knew he wanted me to, and after he basked in his triumph for a minute or so, he stood up and without saying a word, walked back inside. I was so angry at myself for letting him "win." I told myself I needed to be stronger and tougher, so over time, I became stronger and tougher. I didn't want to be. I believed I *had* to be. I told myself I was weak, and I learned to be "strong" by developing a hard, cold exterior. I became somewhat of a bully to other kids I loved and cared about, because being feared and in control was the only way I knew how to keep myself safe.

I'm lucky, because I never hated my inner child in adulthood. I loved her and felt so sorry for her. I wanted to protect her, and I mourned for the child and adult I didn't get to be. I'll never know the version of Heidi I would have become if I hadn't endured so much childhood trauma. I long to know her, and I'm so sad I never will. Because of this, I developed empathy for my child self during my teenage years, but I hated my adult self—this "disgusting, unlovable person" I became because my childhood was so terrible. I believed that I was broken and that all my innate potential to be optimistic, kind, gentle, and happy was permanently destroyed. Instead, I became an angry teen and young adult, ready to fight anyone and everyone I perceived as a threat.

Somewhat ironically, in middle school, I was intensely bullied by the school's "mean girls." It was so bad that at one point, I resigned to eating lunch in a bathroom stall because the girls convinced everyone in my grade to shun me from sitting at their table. The scariest of the mean girls physically threatened me a few times, and just like with my stepdad, I went cold, shut down, and told myself what a loser I was because people didn't like me. I felt too small, alone, and weak to protect myself.

In eighth grade, an absolute angel came to me in the form of a friend named Jodi. I honestly might have had my first suicide attempt in middle school if Jodi hadn't found and rescued me. She didn't give a crap about the mean girls, and she defended and protected me from them at every turn. At thirteen years old, she was the first person in my life who ever offered me support and protection when I needed it.

I'm sure it was Jodi's strength and protection that allowed me to become a better advocate for myself in high school. Of course, so much damage had already been done. My parents had divorced when I was four. My dad was fun-loving and smart, and I adored everything about him. Unfortunately for me, he was an airline pilot and thought it was a good idea to move to Guam when he discovered my mom and future stepdad were having an affair.

My dad didn't come back to live in my hometown until I started high school. He lived out of state for most of my childhood. He remarried and started a new family, and outside of holidays and summer vacations, my father's presence was nonexistent during my young life. As you might imagine, this created a lot of pain for me as a child and adolescent. When I was in elementary school, I tried so many times to tell Dad what was happening at home. I didn't have the language or cognitive abilities to say, "I'm being abused." I didn't even know my mom was an alcoholic until I was in high school. I wish I had known she was always drunk; I just thought she was a ding-dong.

I couldn't explain anything to my dad in a way that made him take me seriously. I tried many times to tell him how mean my stepfather was and how much I hated living with him, but Dad dismissed me completely. Maybe he was truly incapable of picking up on my many efforts to get his help, or maybe he just couldn't be bothered because he was busy with his new life. When I was an adult, Dad told me he would have done something if he had known about the abuse and basically blamed me for not doing a good enough job explaining it to him. I responded, "You don't get to move away and absolve yourself of all responsibility. You were my dad. It was your job to know. It wasn't my job as a young, abused child to figure out how to get you to take me seriously." I digress.

Back to adolescence, my dad finally decided to move back home the year I started high school, and I immediately moved in with him and his new family. Much to my chagrin, his wife was "totally insane" (how I described her in adolescence), and I experienced an entirely new level of abuse from her, which my dad failed to protect me from, *again*. At least I wasn't afraid of my stepmom in all her craziness, so hers was the abuse I chose to endure.

As my home life continued to be wrought with dysfunction, I searched for love and acceptance in dysfunctional ways and found myself pregnant at fifteen years old. To my parents' credit, when they learned I was pregnant, they offered to help in every way they could as I raised my child. Twenty-one days after my sweet sixteen birthday, my precious daughter was born.

Alex became the light of my life. She was pure and beautiful. She needed me as much as I needed her. Caring for her gave me purpose and a sense of unconditional love I had not yet known. That was a responsibility no newborn should carry. It was not her job to make me feel loved and important. It was my job to bestow those gifts upon her. I really tried. I got up at night to give her bottles. I woke up in the dark of early morning to take her to daycare before I went to high school. I held her, kissed her, read to her, and played with her in between doing my homework and trying to be an ordinary sixteen-year-old. I really did "try my best."

Unfortunately for Alex, my best was sometimes just not good enough. I couldn't care for myself at sixteen, so I often failed in caring for her. She was a colicky baby who needed extra love and attention. Sometimes she needed more than I had to give. I got frustrated. I became exhausted from hours of walking and bouncing her to soothe her upset tummy. I sometimes let her "cry it out" in her electronic baby swing when I couldn't handle the responsibility anymore.

I knew nothing of child development. My dad bragged about how he had trained me to sleep through the night as an infant by ignoring the cries and screams from my crib. I didn't know then what "crying it out" did to an infant's developing brain. My parents didn't know either. I know now that allowing a baby to cry alone for long periods teaches them they cannot get their needs met. They eventually stop crying because they give up hope that someone will come to help them. It can make them anxious and untrusting, and it interferes with their ability to self-soothe. I wish I knew that then. I made so many mistakes with lasting consequences.

The reality was, Alex and I lived in a highly dysfunctional household. I did not have the power at sixteen to shield Alex from all the unhealthy dynamics that existed in our home. I was tired, overwhelmed, and a naturally self-centered adolescent. Try as I might, there was only so much I had to give. I knew I needed to get out of my family home as soon as I could, but my self-esteem was abysmal. I doubted my ability to find love or care for myself independently.

Truth be told, I put far too much weight on the importance of finding a partner. I wish I had the gift of feminism back then so I could have seen myself as powerful and capable, independent of a romantic relationship. Such was not my life at the time. I thought the best I could hope for was to marry a nice man who would take good care of me. As a teen mom, I felt like damaged goods, and my expectations for myself and my life were woefully low. When I was twenty years old, I married the older brother of a high school friend, not so much for love but for security. I always envied my friend for her loving family. I wanted Alex to be part of a "good family" too.

I was married for nearly seven years and had two other daughters with my husband before we divorced. It was a tumultuous marriage from the beginning, and had it not been for my deep insecurities, it never would have lasted as long as it did. I was twenty-seven years old when I finally had enough internal strength to say to myself, "I am still young and capable of creating a life much happier than this. I don't have to be miserable here forever." I left, and as painful as it was, I know I freed both myself and my husband from a very unhappy life.

Suddenly, I was a single mom of three children, working full time. Despite my best efforts to foster self-worth, I was still plagued with insecurity. Being a divorced twenty-something with three children only heightened my belief that I was unlovable. I was overwhelmed with responsibility, pressure, self-doubt, and loneliness. I became severely depressed. My ex-husband found love quickly after our split, but I struggled considerably, latching onto unhealthy relationships and getting consumed by them.

I was so consumed in my own agony and self-loathing, I barely attended to my children's emotional needs. They were suffering through their parents' divorce, and I was so blinded by my own pain I couldn't even see it. Because I was tragically unprotected as a child, I believed if I protected my children from being abused, I would be doing a good job as their mom. I was missing the mark by a long shot, and at some point, I started to realize it.

I was obsessed with finding a new partner to make me feel whole and worthy again. I felt like a failure in love, a failure as a mother, and a failure as a provider because I dropped out of college and saw myself as incapable of financially supporting my children. I was on welfare, and I felt like the grossest, dumbest, worst human alive. I believed my children would be better off being raised by their father and new stepmother than having to deal with their basket case of a mother ruining their lives.

I attempted to end my life. I won't tell this story because like all suicide attempts, it gets a little gruesome and I know how triggering these kinds of stories can be for complex trauma survivors. I share this piece only because I want you to know how profound the depths of my self-hatred became. This very serious threat to my life ended with my ex-husband getting emergency custody of our children, and I was required to get court-ordered therapy if I wanted my equal parenting time back. While this was absolutely the most devastating, humiliating thing I ever went through, it was also the greatest thing that ever happened to me because at twenty-eight years old, I finally went to therapy for the first time.

Therapy changed my life in immeasurable ways. I began healing my inner child and loving my adult self despite all the mistakes I made. I accepted and (mostly) forgave myself for how much I screwed up or hurt the people I love, especially my daughters. I was inspired to go to graduate school and spent the next decade of my life completing my bachelor's through doctorate degrees.

My therapy experience changed me so much that I felt compelled to give back by becoming a psychologist myself. I was blessed with so many gifts along the way. I had incredible mentors who helped me become an excellent trauma therapist (I mean, how amazing is it that I can even confidently announce that I know I'm great at what I do? Huge win!). The worst moment of my life set me on an incredible, transformative journey that continues to amaze me nearly twenty years later.

I was lucky that my healing journey led to self-love. As I've already stated, I don't always love myself. I still occasionally go back to that dark, self-hating place. When I do, I fall back into my old pattern of telling myself what a worthless piece of shit I am. The difference now is I don't go there nearly as often as I used to, and when those ugly voices come back into my head, I know they are liars. I say to myself, "This is just my depression talking. I know this isn't the truth and I know this terrible feeling will eventually pass and be replaced by a better feeling, because it always does. I just need to wait it out and not do anything to make it worse."

I give myself permission to order takeout, binge-watch my favorite funny television shows, and do literally whatever I need to do to get through the depression and get to the other side. When it's especially bad, it can take several days. I know I'm supposed to reach out to friends and move my body and do other healthy self-care things, but like you, sometimes I just can't. So, I show myself compassion, I give myself grace, and I start going on walks and reaching out just as soon as I feel able. I don't beat myself up for not responding perfectly to my depression. I am gentle with myself because, eventually, I always find my way out of it. Always.

This is a good time to mention *why* I think I was able to find self-love and why it might be different for other childhood trauma survivors. In my case, while I experienced a lot of childhood trauma, I also experienced a lot of childhood joy. I believed I was smart, talented, and pretty as a young girl. I believed these things because both my biological parents said them to me regularly. I had two abusive stepparents who hated me, and though my parents didn't protect me from them, I still felt loved by and important to each of my parents.

My mom did a great job getting me involved in extracurricular activities. I participated in Girl Scouts, choir, dance, and theater. I was smart and got good grades in school. Despite my bullying experiences, I liked school and usually felt like I had friends who cared about me. I lived in a safe neighborhood and my basic needs were always met. We even went on regular vacations and there were plenty of opportunities for me to have fun. These protective factors made all the difference in the world.

You may relate to having two parts battling it out inside you: a healthy part that knows you have worth and value and can accomplish something good in the world, as well as a traumatized part that tells you how worthless, stupid, and unlovable you are.

Your work is to befriend the healthy part, no matter how tiny it feels in comparison to the big, loud, and traumatized part. You will need to nurture that little voice until it grows bigger, gets stronger, and eventually becomes the primary voice inside your head.

CHAPTER 2

How Complex Trauma Sticks with You

In the book's introduction, I refer to both "childhood trauma" and "complex trauma." You've probably heard these two terms used in many contexts throughout your own life. While I may use them interchangeably for the purposes of this book, they do have an important distinction:

- *Childhood trauma* is exactly what it sounds like: traumatic events that occur during a person's childhood. These can be single traumatic events, infrequent traumas, or regularly occurring traumas.

- *Complex trauma* is a little more, well, complex. Complex trauma occurs when trauma is so significant, and repeated so frequently, that a child cannot escape it. It requires a child to create belief systems and coping mechanisms to deal with the seemingly unending trauma. Almost always, the child experiences so much shame and hopelessness because of their trauma that it's impossible for them to grow up having a strong sense of self-worth.

Understanding Childhood Trauma

Children are naturally self-centered, so when good things happen to them, they assume it is because they are good. Likewise, when bad things happen to them, they assume it is because they are bad. Children need adults to help them make sense of the bad things that happen to and around them so that they don't internalize these things as their fault. Children have an enormous capacity for coping with trauma if they have healthy caretakers who help them feel safe and loved when something bad happens.

For a child living through complex trauma, there is usually an inadequate amount of love, safety, and security for them to work through the bad stuff in a healthy way. They come to believe that bad things happen to them because they are not good enough, unlovable, or inherently bad and unworthy of care and protection. As a result, these children often grow to be adults who believe there is something deeply wrong with them. They blame themselves for their trauma and abuse; they feel as if they are broken and need to hide away from the rest of society. They avoid true connection and vulnerability with others because they believe they are monsters, and they don't want anyone else to discover the "truth" about them. It is a perpetual cycle of shame, emotional pain, and self-loathing.

A child who lived through trauma or abuse will almost always experience negative consequences that impact them in adulthood. They will hold untrue beliefs about themselves, have poor coping skills, display unhealthy relationship patterns, and struggle with mental health issues. If they were lucky to have some mitigating factors in childhood—like an adult who made them feel loved and safe, strong ties to their community, or an opportunity to excel in school or in extracurricular activities—they may get to adulthood and still have the capacity for self-love. But not always.

However, a child who lived through *complex trauma* in particular will have a more difficult time. For them, there were often few breaks from the trauma, no significant mitigating factors, and no opportunity to develop a healthy or realistic view of themselves. These survivors feel lost in adulthood and may have little identity at all outside their assumed role of being bad or broken. With that knowledge, it's understandable that a complex trauma survivor wouldn't have the capacity for self-love. You can see why all those messages about "just loving yourself as you are" fall flat for survivors of complex trauma—it's about as easy for them as speaking a brand new language with no exposure to it at all.

Another important distinction related to childhood trauma is that some people still equate all trauma with posttraumatic stress disorder (PTSD). They believe that unless you are diagnosed with PTSD, you didn't experience trauma. Nothing could be further from the truth. Trauma occurs anytime a person is exposed to an extremely upsetting event (or series of events) that leaves them with troubling aftereffects. As stated earlier, trauma can occur anytime bad things happen, and you can't control or stop them. Yes, all people experience hardships, pain, and moments of suffering and, no, that does not mean everyone is a trauma survivor. The important distinction lies in how a person reconciles what happened to them and moves forward once it's over. For children, their outcomes depend largely on what kind of support they receive from the adults in their life.

For example, I have a friend who is a social worker. She's a great mom, and being a mental health professional gives her an advantage in attending to and understanding the emotional needs of her daughter, who asked to be called Zuri for the purposes of this story.

When I was doing research for my previous book on self-love, I conducted an experiment with some of my friends and their young children. I asked friends with kindergarteners and below to ask their children, "What do you love about yourself?" and record their answers.

It was a fun exercise, and I received many adorable answers, but Zuri's answer really stood out. Her response was "I can stand up for myself and other people." It was a powerful answer from a kindergartener, so her mom gave me some context. Earlier that week, a boy at school said to Zuri, "I don't like Black people." Zuri's father is Black, her mom is Latina, and obviously this was a devastating thing for a little girl to hear from one of her peers. Because Zuri had a parent whom she trusted would help her in times of distress, she immediately told her mom what happened when she arrived home from school, and here is where it got interesting.

Zuri's mother told her it was unacceptable for anyone to say anything ugly about her, especially about her skin color. She went to the school the next day and told Zuri's teacher what happened. Zuri's teacher called the boy's parents. The boy was reprimanded and apologized for his cruel words. Zuri walked away from this potentially traumatic incident, one that might have been the beginning of a lifetime of insecurity and self-doubt, with her head held high and a new sense of empowerment. She also noted one of the things she loved about herself was her "hair and skin color, no matter what." Zuri was not traumatized by this painful experience because she got exactly what she needed from her mother and the other adults in this situation, allowing her to properly reconcile it and move on.

A close family friend also had young children when I ran this experiment, and her youngest son provided another interesting response. He noted that he loved himself because he was "nice to everyone all the time." Now, he was a typical preschooler who could be ornery, unreasonable, and naturally selfish, as young children are. In fact, until around the age of four or five, children cannot perceive the world in any way other than through their own eyes. This is why young children believe good things happen to them because they are good, and bad things happen to them because they are bad. This child lived in a world where all the adults around him *were* nice to him, even if he was throwing a tantrum or otherwise being a little stinker. He internalized the kindness of others as a reflection of himself and believed he, too, was nice to everyone all the time, even though it wasn't *quite* true.

These examples illuminate the fragility of the young human mind. Adults have great influence over the children they raise because so much brain development happens in childhood, especially in the first six or seven years of a child's life. Therefore, much of a person's template for how they see themselves, others, and the world is developed in those early years. If a child develops a belief that they are bad, unlovable, stupid, and so forth, and serious intervention does not occur while they are still young, chances are high that those beliefs will get reinforced over and over and become strongly held beliefs by the time they reach adulthood.

The Negativity Bias

Once these negative beliefs take hold, it can be extremely difficult to let them go. Over time, the beliefs will filter into all their human interactions, including their work, home, and social interactions—and especially into their overall mental health. You can see how a person who lived through chronic childhood trauma might find the concept of self-love preposterous when it is presented as something they "need" to do to heal. Often, people don't even know their childhood trauma is the cause of their self-loathing. They might come into therapy and say, "I don't ever think about that stuff anymore," as if that means none of it impacts them in the present. Unfortunately, you don't need to think about your childhood trauma for it to have a devastating impact on your self-concept as an adult.

As humans, we often give more weight to the negative messages we receive than the positive ones. Psychologists refer to this as the *negativity bias*. There is an adaptive function to this human condition. Let's say you have a hundred good or neutral experiences with a dog. Then, you have one experience in which a dog unexpectedly bites you and causes significant injury. This one experience is going to supersede the many others you've had. This cognitive function is not always a bad thing—it serves to protect you. You *need* to remember the negative experience more intensely so you can protect yourself in similar circumstances in the future. Your brain wants you to put that "bad" experience in the forefront of your mind so you can keep yourself safe around other dogs you encounter in your life. It's easy to see the adaptive survival mechanism at play in the negativity bias. It keeps us alive, so it's a good thing, but it also creates challenges for us.

The biggest challenge with the negativity bias is that our brains are not sophisticated enough to distinguish between physical danger and emotional danger. If children on the school bus call you a "loser" because your parents can't afford to buy you designer clothes, that experience is going to cause emotional pain. Your brain wants you to remember the painful message so you can develop skills to protect yourself from being called hurtful names in the future. The inner critic is born from that desire to protect yourself. Your brain thinks it can keep you safe from the criticism and rejection of others if it constantly points out all the things that might be wrong with you. It repeatedly sends you messages about what you need to do differently to make yourself worthy and likable. Your brain thinks it is helping you, but this thinking is flawed.

Trusting your inner critic can make you an adult with a chip on your shoulder, always trying to prove to others that you aren't a loser, because deep down you think you are. Perhaps you become an adult who finds your weaknesses intolerable. You may be perfectionistic, overly demanding, and highly self-critical. Maybe you push yourself to be the best in everything you do because anything less than perfect is a failure by your standards. Only when you have the best job, buy the best house, drive the best car, and wear the best clothes, will you convince yourself that you aren't the "loser" kid you once were on the school bus.

The sad truth is, no amount of external proof will ever convince you that you aren't a loser, because you already believe you are. You could become an unfillable pit of self-doubt and insecurity, desperately looking for the next thing to fill you up and make you feel temporarily "good enough." Unfortunately, you will just be chasing an insatiable thirst for the rest of your life if you can't learn to fill your wound with some form of self-acceptance. Notice I didn't say "self-love" because that really isn't the thing you need.

You'll need to decipher the many voices in your head and filter out the voices of your past that speak with hateful words and unkind tones: "You're never going to be successful at that. You're so stupid. I can't believe you said that. Nobody likes you. Just give up." Whose voice is that? It isn't yours. Children aren't born thinking that way about themselves. Your original voice is one of love, encouragement, and determination. It is a voice of kindness, assuredness, and gentle strength. It may be buried way down deep. It may have been silent for many years, or maybe you don't remember it existing at all. That's okay. It's still in there. We're going to find it.

Finding Your Inner Voice

You may be wondering, "How do I know which voice is mine? How do you know my original inner voice was kind and loving?" All you need to do to answer this question is spend a little time with a child whose original voice has not yet been tainted by the outside world. One of the sweetest representations of a child's pure delight in themselves is a once-viral video titled "Jessica's Daily Affirmation." I have uploaded the video for your viewing pleasure to my website, drheidigreen.com. It features an adorable young girl with curly blonde hair talking to herself in the mirror. Sweet Jessica says to herself with enthusiasm, "I like my hair! I like my pajamas! I like my whole house! I can do anything good!" Jessica still has her original voice. Her inner voice tells her she is beautiful, strong, capable, and kind.

Many years ago, when I was a preschool teacher, I saw the innate self-love of children daily. To see it, I could just ask the children about their talents. Young children will almost always tell you they are good at things with which they have little to no experience. "Who is a great artist?" Hands go flying up. "Who is a fast runner?" Hands shoot up again. Children are excited to show off their capabilities no matter what their skill level. Every "Hey, Mom, watch this!" kid at the park or public swimming pool can prove that point. The human mind is designed to love and encourage itself, to believe in its capabilities and approach life with enthusiasm and wonder. Some of that inborn, positive mindset is lost to societal conditioning and other typical life experiences, but we can lose detrimental amounts of it when we experience trauma.

People sometimes think the critical voice in their head is a motivating factor. When I speak of self-kindness, clients often tell me they need their harsh internal voice to motivate them, to keep them from becoming lazy or complacent. I challenge this belief right away with a hypothetical scenario.

Let's say you are tasked with teaching a young child to ride a bike. What is your approach? Likely, you will begin with a little pep talk: "Riding a bike is fun! You are so big! You can do it!" Then you will sprinkle in some understanding around the child's uncertainty and offer support: "I will be right here the whole time. I'll hold the back of the seat so you don't fall until you can do it on your own." Once the child is up and riding, you offer an enthusiastic celebration: "You're doing it! You're a great bike rider!" Then, when the inevitable first fall happens, you offer both compassion and encouragement: "Are you okay? Let me clean the scratch. You were doing so well. Sometimes falls happen. Don't worry. You can get back up and try again when you're ready. I'm proud of you!"

When we are our best adult selves, we don't motivate children by criticizing and insulting them. We don't say to them, "Listen, dummy. Riding a bike is easy. Just get up and do it!" Why don't we speak that way? *Because our innate wisdom tells us the way to encourage someone to succeed is to do it through love, not insults, threats, or shame.*

The response I sometimes get next is "Well, yes, that might work for a child, but I'm an adult. I'm not going to coddle myself like that." I follow up with "How do you motivate and encourage a friend?" When you are being a good friend, you offer motivation and encouragement, not unlike you would to a child. You follow a similar script, which includes sharing your belief in them and offering empathy for their doubts and fear. Then you express encouragement and enthusiasm in their favor. We don't motivate our friends with disparaging remarks about what a failure they will be if they can't get it right. We don't tell them they aren't smart enough or talented enough. We don't say to our friends, "Just give up. You don't have what it takes."

Think back for a moment to the most valuable mentors you've had in your adult life. Whether a boss, professor, coach, or even a therapist, they each had a positive impact on you because they motivated you with kindness. We value those who believe in us when we don't believe in ourselves. People who offer us guidance, support, and encouragement when we struggle to master it for ourselves are the ones we look back on with fondness and gratitude.

In her outstanding book, *Animals Make Us Human*, Dr. Temple Grandin discusses how distress impedes learning in animals, just as it does in humans. All mammals innately feel rage, panic, and fear. These emotional experiences interfere with learning and brain development. Similarly, we know that pressure, criticism, and humiliation from others make us nervous and interrupt learning. But when talking to ourselves, we can get confused. We might use self-criticism to get something done, and when we succeed (despite the criticism), we falsely associate self-criticism with effective motivation.

However, in our hearts, we know positive inspiration is the best motivator. It's why we give it to others. It's why we value the people who offer it to us. So why do we fail to give it to ourselves?

People often talk to themselves in ways they would never speak to another human being. I'm guilty of this as well. I have been terribly unkind to myself, more so than I would be to a person I seriously disliked. There is only one explanation. That is not my voice. I know my voice. I hear it every day to every person I encounter. I am not unkind. I am a good-natured person. My voice is gentle. The ugly noise that shows up in my head belongs to someone else. Likewise, the unloving voice in your head is not yours. It has been planted there by people and experiences that were painful. It is your duty to yourself to reject that voice entirely so you can benefit from the same loving-kindness you offer others.

CHAPTER 3

Get Real About Your Trauma Origin Story

When I ask clients to talk to me about their past, it's not unusual for me to get some pushback. Going back and reliving painful memories can be very difficult. But these stories are indeed important. I encourage clients to verbalize their "origin stories" because, just like in the movies, understanding the backstory is crucial to understanding what is happening in the story now.

Why does your trauma origin story matter? Because our traumatic life experiences color our belief systems about ourselves, others, and the world. Years after childhood trauma is over, even when we "never think about it anymore," and even if we think we're "over it," the lessons we learned through our trauma remain in the unconscious parts of the brain. Our brains constantly scan for danger and pay close attention to any new experience that seems even somewhat like our old traumatic experiences. It's responsible for giving us "gut feelings" that might be incredibly helpful in keeping us safe but might also fool us into thinking there's a present threat when there isn't (more on that later).

Unconscious memories not only keep us safe, but they also supply the foundation for which we see ourselves. Built upon that foundation is our sense of self-worth, our beliefs about what kind of person we are, and our beliefs about how we should expect to be treated by others. When we experience complex trauma in childhood, all these beliefs get skewed, and they interfere with almost every aspect of how we view ourselves and our experiences. In the next section, I'll give you an example of how this looked for a client I'll call Alma.

Alma's Story

Alma was in her early thirties when she decided she could no longer live with the depression, crippling negative self-talk, and self-doubt that dominated her thoughts and decision-making. Growing up in a Hispanic culture, she did not believe childhood trauma could be the root of her mental health problems. She was taught that family matters should stay in the family and not be discussed with outsiders. It was hard for her to come to therapy and share her mental health concerns with a stranger. She described her childhood as "mostly good" when she came to therapy for the first time, but she also acknowledged some early life experiences that were quite challenging. It took a while for Alma to feel comfortable talking about the specifics because she did not want to "betray" her parents. This is quite common with childhood trauma survivors.

Alma's father coached her soccer and softball teams when she was in middle school. While she was a talented athlete just like he had been at her age, she mostly had memories of him being exceptionally hard on her when it came to her performance. Alma recalled how her father screamed at her on the field, embarrassing her in front of her peers. She noted that even though she was the strongest athlete on the team, her father often appeared frustrated, disappointed, and outright angry at her any time she failed to score or had the ball stolen by another player.

At home, his treatment of her was even worse. Sometimes her father would say things like “I am disgusted with you” or “You humiliated me out there today.” At times, he wouldn’t speak to her for days after she disappointed him in some way, even when she believed the “mistake” she made was relatively small.

Alma eventually acknowledged her father ruined her love of sports, and she dreaded participating in these types of events because she knew it would likely lead to emotional abuse from him. Of course, Alma never used the term *emotional abuse* to describe the way he treated her. She acknowledged that he made her feel as though nothing she ever did was good enough. He made her feel small. She knew the only way for her to win her father’s love or approval was to be perfect in every way, but she didn’t initially see that as abuse. It was just how it was in their household.

Alma went on to describe how her mother responded to her father’s behavior. She noted that despite going to her mother for validation and comfort when she was young, her mom always defended the actions of her father. She said things like “He just wants you to be the best,” “It’s important to listen to him and make him proud,” and “He is only hard on you because he loves you.”

Eventually, Alma stopped seeking support from her mother and became very isolated in her home. She spent many hours alone in her room, feeling like a failure and a disappointment. She became incredibly unhappy with herself, believing the abuse she received was justified because she was letting her father down.

Moreover, she listened to her father scream at her mother in ways similar to how he screamed at her. He called her mom stupid and worthless. He told her she would be nothing without him. To Alma's knowledge, he never struck her mother, but he was violent in other ways. He threw objects, punched holes in the wall, broke things, and on more than one occasion, kicked the family dog. Alma was afraid of her father. Everyone in the house was afraid of him.

The combination of her father's mistreatment and her mother's complicity taught her that criticism and cruelty are expressions of love. The statement "He is only hard on you because he loves you" led Alma to expect those who care about her to continually judge, condemn, and disapprove of her. Accordingly, she not only developed an internal dialogue that was hateful and demeaning, but she came to expect that sort of treatment from others.

As an adult, Alma found herself terrified of making mistakes. She sought validation and approval from her parents, friends, colleagues, romantic partners, and everyone else in her life. She was unable to make decisions for herself without consulting multiple sources to make sure she was doing the "right" thing. She didn't trust herself to make good decisions because she believed she was incapable of getting things right on her own.

Alma accepted poor treatment from others in her life. She worked at a job where she was taken advantage of and treated poorly by her boss. She had a slew of failed romantic relationships, which, interestingly, she *did* describe as abusive. She noted that her former partners were demeaning, made her feel worthless, and were sometimes physically abusive. She added that she didn't know why she kept attracting partners who treated her so poorly, but she believed "that's just how men are." She did not believe she deserved better treatment despite wanting more respect and kindness in her relationships.

At first, Alma did not connect her insecurities or poor relationship patterns to her childhood experiences. In fact, she was very hesitant to accept that her emotional struggles in adulthood might be attributable to mistakes her parents made in their parenting. "They loved me," "They did the best they could," and "I don't want to blame them" were phrases she repeated time and again throughout her treatment. Alma could not reconcile that a parent who loved her might also have abused her. She believed her father's love for her made all his harmful behavior acceptable, and for a long time she was adamant that her poor self-image was her fault. She believed she was a disappointing child, and she believed she was a disappointment as an adult.

A Faulty Belief System

As you can see, it's natural for a child to determine they are the problem when adults are unkind to them. By all accounts, Alma was a talented athlete who had every right to feel good about herself and proud of her abilities. Because her father's emotional abuse began when she was young and her brain was still forming, it was difficult for her to let go of his programming in her adulthood.

It can be difficult for complex trauma survivors to acknowledge where their distorted beliefs come from because, often, people want to protect their parents, even when their parents have done incredible harm to them. Indeed, Alma rarely thought about her parents' mistreatment of her. She didn't even see it as mistreatment. Because she did not want to acknowledge the ways in which her parents had failed her, she clung to the idea that she was the problem, which made treatment difficult in the early stages.

Eventually, though, Alma was willing to see how her parents had created a faulty belief system in her as a child, which made it difficult for her to love herself in adulthood. Her father's abuse instilled in her the idea that something was wrong with her, while her mother's dismissal of his abuse taught her that it was acceptable for people who love you to tear you down and treat you poorly.

Like all children, Alma was a child worthy of love and affection from her parents. Had she been the recipient of healthy parenting, she likely would have grown to be full of confidence and self-love. It was crucial for Alma to acknowledge that her childhood trauma was to blame for her poor self-worth. If she couldn't acknowledge her self-loathing was created from a dysfunctional experience, she may never have been able to acknowledge that the ugly thoughts she had about herself were untrue. She may have spent her entire life insisting that she was unworthy simply because she felt unworthy. To see the truth about herself, she needed to get real about her trauma story. You will too.

The first step is to think back to the messages you took in about yourself as a child. Ideally, you received plenty of positive affirmations about how smart, talented, and capable you were. If that were true, though, I don't imagine you would be reading this book. It's likely that even if you did get some healthy messaging about yourself early in life, you also received unhealthy and untrue messages about yourself. These messages are often subtle and enter your identity without conscious awareness, as not all abuse is overt like Alma's was. Some abuse is covert, meaning it is so subtle that it is nearly undetectable. Victims of covert abuse often think the abuse is normal behavior, or they can be easily convinced to accept it from their perpetrators.

If you are a survivor of covert abuse, you may struggle to understand why you feel so terrible about yourself. Perhaps you had a mother who made off-handed comments about what you ate and who praised other children for how thin they were. Maybe you had a parent who seemed completely uninterested in you, and nothing you did could ever win you the affection you longed for. Maybe you were raised by someone who took credit for all your achievements and made you feel like you were only successful because of them.

There are many forms of covert abuse, and they can sometimes be more difficult to sort through than overt abuse because it's so challenging to separate yourself from the negative beliefs you hold about you. No matter what kind of negative messages you received about yourself in childhood (whether verbal or nonverbal), identifying your underlying core beliefs and recognizing what external forces put those ideas in your head is the first step in moving from self-loathing to self-neutrality.

Making Peace with Childhood Trauma

The bottom line is that childhood messages create the inner voice we take with us into adulthood. They become the foundation on which other beliefs about ourselves, others, and the world around us are laid. In addition, as we move through life, we seek to confirm or reject messages we get about ourselves and our environment.

There was a groundbreaking research project conducted in Southern California through the Centers for Disease Control and Prevention (CDC) and Kaiser Permanente in the late 1990s that helped researchers understand how devastating early traumatic experiences can be on a developing child. Known as the Adverse

Childhood Experiences (ACE) Study, this project included over 17,000 participants who provided personal information used to link traumatic childhood experiences to mental and physical health problems later in adulthood. The survey consisted of ten questions that fell into three different categories: abuse, neglect, and household dysfunction. Three questions asked about abuse: physical, emotional, and sexual. Two questions asked about neglect: physical and emotional. The remaining five questions asked about household dysfunction, specifically: if your parents had ever divorced or separated, if either of your parents had a mental illness or substance abuse problem, if you had a family member who was incarcerated, or if there was violence between the adults in your home. This last set of questions is important because it shows that you don't have to be a victim of child abuse or neglect to experience long-standing health issues directly correlated to your early home life.

Based on participants' answers to these questions, they received an ACE score that reflected how many traumatic childhood experiences they had endured. The results were staggering. There was a direct correlation between the number of ACEs a person had experienced and their physical and mental health in adulthood. Not only did the study find that the more ACEs someone has, the more significant their risk of physical and mental health issues later in life, but it also revealed that the presence of even one ACE is enough to change a person's long-term health outcomes. This means that even if you had a relatively happy childhood, if your parents fought all the time or were divorced, or if one of your parents drank too much, you've got an ACE. Even one ACE likely changed your belief system about yourself, others, and the world. Ultimately, it may have shifted your feelings of self-worth and self-love enough to change the trajectory of your life.

I don't mean to scare you with these statistics. As a fellow survivor of childhood trauma, I have an ACE score of five, which means I am at significant risk for a whole host of ailments. One risk factor, teen pregnancy, drastically changed my life, but I continue to be at risk as an adult for other conditions such as depression, anxiety, alcoholism, drug addiction, suicide, cancer, liver disease, sexually transmitted diseases, domestic violence, obesity, stroke, heart disease, rape, and more. Whew. So that's the bad news.

But the good news is despite struggling with a handful of those risk factors, I've made peace with my childhood experiences thanks to the help of some great therapists. I'm in good physical health and enjoy generally good emotional health as well. I have learned to practice neutrality toward myself (most of the time), and when self-loathing creeps back in (which it does), I have good skills to neutralize those ugly voices. I'm a productive, well-educated member of society. I have (mostly) healthy relationships with the important people in my life. I'm happy and peaceful most of the time, despite the significant history of childhood trauma I endured.

Thankfully, positive childhood experiences help mitigate the aftereffects of childhood trauma. For example, as a counterpart to the ACE Study, researchers developed a corresponding scale to measure positive childhood experiences, called the Benevolent Childhood Experiences (BCEs) Scale. Though it hasn't yet been studied on the grand scale of the original ACE Study, the BCEs Scale was designed specifically for adults who survived high levels of childhood adversity.

The BCEs Scale assesses the presence of ten positive childhood experiences, such as love, predictability, and support. Some questions included on the scale are "Did you like school?" "Did you have at least one good friend?" and "Did you have at least one teacher who cared about you?" Just like the ACE Survey, the BCEs Scale produces a score of one to ten. However, because this study didn't follow participants from childhood through adulthood like the ACE Study did, it was not able to measure the multitude of physical ailments that are attributable to childhood trauma. However, it could show how favorable childhood experiences reduce psychological symptoms in adulthood.

For example, people with high BCEs reported lower levels of psychological distress in adulthood, including lower levels of depression, PTSD symptoms, and overall stress. In my case, I have a BCEs score of nine, so while I still struggled with some of the mental health and social struggles of people with high ACE scores (depression, teen pregnancy, and a suicide attempt), my high BCEs score also allowed me to develop a healthy sense of self in addition to a traumatized self.

The moral of the story is no matter what your ACE score, you are not a hopeless case. You may have more challenges to overcome than a person with a lower score, but you are still fully capable of having a satisfying life and a peaceful heart. If you are interested in finding out your ACE score, you can visit my website at drheidigreen.com to take the survey and learn more.

CHAPTER 4

Acceptance as a Path to Self-Neutrality

I know, I've probably dropped a lot of hard stuff on you in just three chapters. If you experienced childhood trauma, especially if you haven't thought about or processed that trauma in a long time, you might be feeling overwhelmed. At this point, you might be realizing why self-love feels impossible for you. Moreover, I hope you are becoming open to the truth that self-love seems out of reach because of the things that happened *to* you, not because of who you are. It's not your fault.

Sometimes people have a very hard time accepting this truth. In therapy, I ask clients to imagine a child they know and love who is around the same age they were when the abuse or trauma occurred. Then I ask, "If what happened to you were to happen to this child you care about, would it be their fault? Would you tell them they are defective and unlovable? Would you tell them they are less worthy because of the abuse they endured?" Of course, no one has ever said yes to this question. We tend to be much kinder to other people than we are to ourselves.

Occasionally, someone will say they don't know any children around the same age as they were at the time, so they can't imagine this scenario. In that case, I ask them to imagine they come across a child who is being abused or traumatized in the same way they were. This time I ask, "If you suddenly were to witness a child who was in the exact situation you were in, would you walk right by thinking they probably deserved it? Would you assume they were being abused because they were unlovable?" Again, everyone says no, so I follow up with "If you came across this child, wouldn't you want to step in and rescue them? Once you got them somewhere safe, what would you want this child to know about what happened to them?" Again, without fail, people express that they would naturally come to the child's rescue.

The point of all of this isn't to force you to relive traumatic experiences. It's to show you that if you have thought you were unlovable your whole life, or if you picked up this book because the thought of loving yourself is a totally foreign concept, it's likely a result of conditioning that happened in childhood. Stepping outside yourself often helps you see things more accurately. I've had several clients who say, "I get that it isn't okay for another child to endure this, and they shouldn't see themselves as unlovable if it happens to them, but it's different for me." When I ask how it's different, often the answer is "I don't know, it just is." People try to convince me that they are different from other children; that those children really are lovable whereas they are not.

If we hit this point in the process, I ask my clients to consider that they might not be so different from every other child on the planet. It isn't likely they are the one exception in humanity to this overarching rule. I will again ask if they can at least be open to the possibility that they feel this way because they were conditioned to feel this way and not because it is true. If you've been reading this section thinking, "Yes, this is me," then I am going to ask you to remain open now. I promise you were not the only child in existence who learned they didn't deserve love because something terrible happened to them. You have nothing to be ashamed of or to feel guilty about.

It's time to embrace the notion that just because you *feel* unlovable, that doesn't mean you are or ever were unlovable. You can acknowledge that your trauma was so intense and started when you were so young that the window for creating self-love might be closed for you. However, you are still capable of happiness, peace, and a content life.

You don't have to believe it yet. You'll get there. In the previous chapter, I mentioned that the first step in moving toward self-neutrality is to identify your underlying core beliefs and where they came from. Once you've done that, the next step is to find the place within you that might be willing to believe something different from what you've always believed about yourself. Perhaps you can identify that little crack in your belief system somewhere in your body. Maybe it's a light peeking through a door or crevasse. For right now, just notice it exists inside you, and we'll see if we can keep coming back to it and slowly let the light in more and more throughout this process.

Radical Acceptance

To move toward this second step of achieving self-neutrality, you must learn to find self-acceptance. I know, easier said than done. But it's only by accepting who you are with compassion and understanding that you can see yourself as worthy of the peace that comes with self-neutrality. Before you can feel self-acceptance, though, you must accept reality. You need to acknowledge universal truths, and you must acknowledge that you are not so different from the rest of humanity that universal truths don't apply to you. They do.

Back in the 1970s, a brilliant psychologist named Dr. Marsha Linehan created dialectical behavior therapy, often referred to as DBT. There are four components of DBT, which are usually taught in the following sequential order: mindfulness, interpersonal effectiveness, distress tolerance, and emotion regulation. I'll talk more about these components later, but for now I want to focus on a term she coined in DBT that is relevant to the notion of self-acceptance. That term is called *radical acceptance*.

Radical acceptance is the practice of accepting everything in your life as it is. That's right. Everything. You might think that is hardly rocket science, but you'd be surprised by how many people increase and perpetuate their suffering because they refuse to accept reality. They stay focused on what "should" be or what "should have" been. They spend hours and hours ruminating and wishing things were different instead of accepting what actually is.

People who accept things *as they are* have a huge advantage when it comes to their general happiness. They experience less suffering. Not because their lives have any less suffering than anyone else's, but because they acknowledge that pain is a part of life. They accept it and don't catastrophize when it happens. They're neutral to it.

I realize this is a downright revolutionary concept for some people, but stick with me. It is possible to ride out suffering like a ship on a stormy sea, knowing the pain exists, but also knowing that the pain isn't forever. It's uncomfortable, maybe even miserable, but it's also *temporary*. People who reject what is unchangeable suffer considerably more because, frankly, the energy required to fight against reality is all-consuming and exhausting.

Let me give you an example of how this could play out in real life. If I get in a car accident and am seriously injured, I have every right in the early phases of my healing to feel despair, grief, anger, and any other emotion that comes up in me. It's also important that I don't get stuck in this stage, because if I do, it will hinder the rest of my healing process. At some point, I need to accept whatever my new reality is, whether it be chronic pain, limited mobility, or physical scars. If I develop PTSD, I will need to accept that reality too. If I stay focused on how unfair everything is, or if I repeatedly play through all the alternative scenarios that didn't happen (for example, if I had just left my house earlier, or if that driver wouldn't have been on their phone) then I will impede the process of healing my PTSD. I can't recover until I accept (1) what happened, (2) what is, and (3) what work is next so I can recover.

In this scenario, the "what happened" is that I was in a serious car accident that wasn't my fault. The "what is" is my new reality, which might include life-altering injuries. Even though I didn't cause the accident, I must accept my new physical limitations and accept that I experienced a trauma that will require therapeutic work. Finally, the "what's next" is I need to go to physical therapy and work with a trauma therapist to give myself the best outcomes, both physically and emotionally.

Don't get me wrong, I am allowed to hate what happened! But I can't allow myself to resist acceptance by focusing on how unfair it was or ruminating about all the what-ifs that didn't happen. My mind and body need me to stay focused on the power I have now for me to heal and recover as fully as possible.

Notice how in both cases, the reality never changes. The accident happens, the injuries occur, and I am left having to do a bunch of work to heal myself when the situation wasn't my fault. Dr. Linehan used to say something like "Your trauma may not be your fault, but healing it is your responsibility." So, with that understanding, I only have two options: (1) Accept reality, try to have a good attitude, and get to healing as quickly as I can, or (2) stay stuck in the initial feelings of despair and anger, refusing to let go of my unhelpful thoughts.

It's human nature to want to imagine things could be or should be different. But the thing you must radically accept is that things *can't* be different. Your traumas happened. You can decide to take all your power back and do what you can to feel better, or you can choose to stay stuck in your pain, perpetuate your suffering, and get in the way of your healing. Only by embracing radical acceptance will you become open to recovery options you didn't think were available.

Focusing on What's in Your Control

As important as it is for your emotional well-being to not fight against reality, it is also important to identify when your circumstances are unacceptable. People who practice radical acceptance are not pushovers. They do not ignore their needs or fail to advocate for themselves. They merely know which battles to fight and how to respond in a healthy way when things are outside their control. And yes, this is also easier said than done!

Let me give you an example. If you are in a relationship with a person who treats you terribly, radical acceptance does not say, "Well, this is just reality. There's nothing I can do about this abusive behavior, so I must accept it." Radical acceptance *does* say, "I cannot control this person's behavior. I cannot change them." It also says, "I don't have to allow it. I can refuse to be in a relationship like this." Radical acceptance means letting go of trying to convince the person to treat you differently. Instead, you accept that their behavior is abusive and that you cannot change it. You recognize that you must act to protect yourself from abusive behavior, even if it means doing something you don't necessarily want to do, like ending the relationship.

Of course, you always have the choice to stay in the relationship and remain miserable. Doing nothing is a choice, but you must recognize you are *choosing* to suffer even though you have other options. There are *always* other options. If you think you have no options, it's only because you haven't thought of or accepted them yet.

Obviously, you don't want to be dramatic and cut off every relationship you have any time someone treats you in a hurtful way. You have choices, but all your options involve controlling *yourself* and not controlling others. You can explain to the person the reasons their behavior upset you and ask them to change their behavior. If this is a well-adjusted person who cares about you, it shouldn't take too much more than that. You can set up boundaries and expectations for how the relationship should function in a way that respects you both. If a person is making apparent, concerted efforts to honor your boundaries, even if they are imperfect along the way, that's probably worth working through.

If you have made your needs known, set clear boundaries and expectations, and the person continues to ignore them, you must accept that this is who they are. This is how they are going to treat you. If you find their behavior unacceptable and don't want to be engaged with a person who treats you like that, then you must do the only thing you have the power to do: find a way to leave.

If this type of thing is brand new to you, start with this mantra: "I can only control myself. My behaviors, reactions, attitudes, and choices are all entirely within my control. Everything else is outside my control, and I must accept what is outside of me." Adopting this attitude can be challenging, I know, but it has led me to more peace than I have ever known in my life.

Like many mental health concepts, radical acceptance is simple in theory, but the learning process can be difficult. Like self-neutrality, it doesn't come naturally. We must train our brains to lean into acceptance. I've been practicing radical acceptance for a long time, and I'm proud to say I've gotten good at it. I've trained my brain to be accepting and kind toward myself. I'm not *always* accepting and kind, to be sure, but I'm much more accepting and kinder than I've been in the past.

When I first started practicing radical acceptance, it was hard. Sometimes I thought it was stupid. I tried to be accepting but it felt contrived, and I got angry. If you find yourself feeling frustrated or annoyed as you begin this practice, try to remember it's to be expected. Anytime you want to train your brain to function in a new way, it is going to feel weird, wrong, awkward, or unhelpful (or all of the above). I promise you can teach yourself healthier ways to operate if you stick with it through the initial challenge.

Perhaps the greatest power of radical acceptance is that it allows you to exist without judging the situation (or your emotions about the situation). That is, you can view your emotions as neither good nor bad and accept that they just *are*. In the car accident example, the grief was painful, but it wasn't wrong or bad. It was a healthy part of the healing process and ultimately a primary component of living in peace. You want to honor and validate your feelings, but you also don't want to get endlessly stuck in them. This is why acceptance is such a crucial part of the healing process.

The Ongoing Work of Radical Self-Acceptance

All this talk of self-acceptance is great in theory, but the truth is, we live in a world that profits from our self-loathing and insecurity. Even if we are intentionally nonjudgmental toward ourselves and others, even if we accept our imperfections and failures as a natural part of the human experience, we still must survive in a media-driven society that continually bombards us with messages of our unworthiness.

If it makes you feel any better, self-acceptance is difficult even for people who have *not* experienced trauma. Think about all the advertisements you see for products or services that alert you to a "problem" in you that you may never have thought about before. Procedures to make your face slimmer, to make your crow's feet less visible, to smooth out your cellulite, to help you lose weight, to help you gain muscle, and on and on to infinity. No matter how much we want to try to accept ourselves, companies make a lot of money ensuring we feel inadequate and unworthy.

Moreover, many advertisers use our desire to love ourselves against us. I see more advertisements than I can count that tell me to buy expensive skin products because "I'm worth it" or that I should subscribe to a monthly fitness app or purchase an eight-dollar bath bomb because "I deserve it." Don't be fooled. Buying expensive skin care products won't make you feel less unworthy. Your self-loathing doesn't stem from not having enough bath bombs. Only *you* can decide what heals your heart, feeds your soul, and honors your worthiness.

Personally, I love world travel, so I save up to take myself on epic adventures. I snap incredible pictures, meet wonderful people, and create priceless memories. That's what my heart longs for, so I decide I am worth it. It's not just the big things either. I can go on sunset walks with my dog, take quiet morning hikes, read a great book, or stream an online yoga class for free. I deserve those simple pleasures too.

You are also deserving, but if you don't feel worthy yet, start by asking yourself what you would do for yourself *if* you felt worthy of treating yourself. Then ease into allowing yourself to do or have the things you would do or have *if* you "deserved them." It's a little bit of "fake it till you make it" here, but to start improving your self-worth, you might just need to behave as if you believe you're worthy.

Your repeated actions will create new neuropathways that will eventually condition your brain to believe in your worth. You can't feel neutral about yourself if you feel unworthy of self-neutrality. So even if you never get to a place of self-love, it still makes sense to treat yourself like a worthwhile human being whose needs matter. Remember, you are not the exception to all of humanity. Everyone deserves to take care of themselves and feel good about it. You are part of everyone, so the rules apply to you too.

CHAPTER 5

Self-Neutrality Through Self-Compassion

Now that you've taken some time to consider your childhood traumas and how they have impacted your view of yourself, it's time to move into a concept that might feel entirely foreign: self-compassion. I have worked with many complex trauma survivors who've never heard the term *self-compassion* until the day I brought it up in therapy. The conversation often goes something like this:

ME: I've noticed you often speak unkindly when you speak about yourself. Perhaps it would be helpful for us to explore how you can be more self-compassionate.

CLIENT: What are you talking about?

ME: I'm saying I think we should focus on building self-compassion.

CLIENT: What is that?

ME: Self-compassion is the idea that you should treat yourself with the same kind of understanding and compassion you have for other people.

CLIENT: I have no idea how to do that.

ME: Well, think about how you react when a person you care about is hurting. If a friend doesn't get a job they applied for, do you tell them it's probably because they're stupid, they suck, and no one likes them?

CLIENT: Of course not.

ME: Okay, but I've noticed when something unpleasant happens to you, you usually respond with extremely harsh words toward yourself. Honestly, you're quite mean to yourself, but you are very caring when it comes to others. Self-compassion is an exercise in treating yourself like a good friend and speaking to yourself the same way you would speak to someone you love when times are difficult and you're feeling bad about yourself.

Frequently, I am met with a scoff and a suggestion that what I'm saying is ridiculous, would be embarrassing, or simply could never work. I don't take it personally. It's natural to respond like this to the concept of self-compassion when you grow up receiving so little compassion from others. Remember that the voices of adults from your childhood become your inner voice in adulthood. If others were harsh, uncaring, or cruel toward you, you naturally became that way toward yourself.

The Self-Compassion Double Standard

Something I've always found interesting is that many people who have terrible negative self-talk are frequently kind to others. They tend to speak to *themselves* the way their abusers spoke to them, but they speak to *others* the way they wish they would have been spoken to in childhood. It's easier to offer kindness to others who are struggling because we intuitively feel compassion for them. We believe that we need to be self-critical to motivate ourselves but see others as needing support if we are to motivate them. It's a flaw in the cognitive system, really.

For example, if a loved one tells you that they are struggling in school, you consider all the other factors in their life that are contributing to this. Maybe they also work a full-time job. Maybe they have stress in their romantic or family life. Maybe their professor has a reputation for being a real hard-ass, or maybe they're having financial difficulties. You examine all the burdens they are carrying and offer empathy for their combined hardships. You understand that they are struggling because of the other circumstances occurring in their life. However, it can be challenging for child abuse survivors to be as objective toward themselves when examining their own difficulties.

Dr. Kristin Neff is a leading psychologist in the realm of self-compassion. Her book *Self-Compassion: The Proven Power of Being Kind to Yourself* was one of the most inspirational reads of my life. In it, Dr. Neff describes three elements of self-compassion: self-kindness, a sense of common humanity, and mindfulness. She describes self-kindness as an act of being warm and understanding toward yourself during periods of suffering or inadequacy, as opposed to flogging yourself with self-criticism and condemnation. In other words, when we understand and expect that failure is a natural part of life, we reduce the suffering we experience during periods of disappointment through self-directed gentleness and acceptance. Self-kindness can make us more likely to try again or find another way to persevere because kindness is encouraging. It builds our resilience and belief in ourselves instead of discouraging and breaking us down.

The next key component of self-compassion—a sense of common humanity—involves acknowledging that pain and feelings of inadequacy are something all humans experience. So often, we feel isolated and alone in our burdens. Knowing that our struggles are part of what connects us to all other people can ease our pain and normalize our experiences. So, the next time you find that you're berating yourself, try saying instead, "I struggle because I am human. Part of the human experience is to feel alone, unsure, and inadequate at times. But I am not alone. My battle to overcome insecurity is one of the things that connects me to all other people. I am imperfect and I struggle just like everyone else."

This type of inner dialogue will help you feel similar to others, rather than isolated and inadequate when you experience pain. The more "normal" you feel, the easier it is to be neutral toward yourself. Self-hatred comes from the belief that we are different and less than all the other people around us. The more we recognize how similar we are to others, the more we can accept ourselves as regular humans living in the human experience. And as you know from the previous chapter, acceptance is key to getting to a place of self-neutrality.

Finally, we can't adequately practice self-compassion without mindfulness. Dr. Neff describes mindfulness as a nonjudgmental state of mind in which feelings are observed neutrally without an effort to change, suppress, or deny them. Essentially, mindfulness allows us to notice our thoughts and feelings without interpreting them as facts. We can accept that just because we perceive something a certain way, it doesn't mean our perception is the truth. When we are open and curious about our internal experiences, we can view them more objectively, without minimizing or exaggerating them. Essentially, we become more self-neutral through intention. Living intentionally requires us to be mindful of our thoughts, emotions, and behaviors.

Self-Compassion in Practice

While practicing the three components of self-compassion is a great way to begin a practice of self-neutrality, I don't want to oversimplify this process. Self-compassion is a challenge for many people. Trauma survivors typically have a difficult time shifting from self-loathing to self-compassion. Some find it intolerable to speak kindly to themselves in the beginning. Self-compassion requires practice and patience. You wouldn't expect to speak fluent Mandarin after one lesson, and you can't expect to be fluent in self-compassion after one lesson either.

You may also feel some guilt right now if you did not identify with the notion of being kinder to others than you are to yourself. Perhaps you read this and thought, "Oh, no. I'm not easier on other people than I am on myself. If anything, I am just as harsh or harsher toward others than I am toward myself!" Let me assure you this is also normal. While some complex trauma survivors are able to offer others the grace they wish they were given as children, other survivors struggle to extend kindness and compassion toward others because they didn't receive it growing up. After all, if you were treated with cruelty during most of your developmental years, you never really learned how to be kind and compassionate.

Remember, everyone responds to traumatic experiences differently, so there isn't a "right" or "wrong" way to end up after surviving childhood trauma.

Mental health practitioners know that childhood trauma looks different for everyone, and the response you have to it depends largely on your specific situation. Please try not to compare yourself to other survivors. Their childhood was different from yours. Their resources and support systems were different. Their strengths, talents, and coping skills were different. It's truly impossible to compare any two complex trauma survivors.

Even siblings who grew up together can have very different experiences in the same house based on a variety of factors, including birth order, family roles and expectations, and differences in temperament and personality. The way you responded to your trauma was the way *you* needed to respond to survive. The struggles you face today absolutely make sense based on *your* experience. You deserve to feel kindness and empathy for the child you were and compassion for the adult you are today.

This is such a difficult concept that even those who do not consider themselves trauma survivors struggle with self-compassion! As such, many of the thought and behavior changes suggested in this book may feel quite unnatural in the beginning. Understand this: Your brain learned to perform in a certain way over the course of many years, and you have repeatedly reinforced that way of thinking throughout your life. Anything that contradicts the way you've been thinking and behaving since you were a child will feel "wrong" at first. Eventually, it will begin to feel healthy and right to be kind to yourself. That's the work of this book—work that I promise will be worth it.

Before we get ahead of ourselves, though, let's spend a little more time exploring why your brain became locked into being unkind to itself in the first place. We will do this by considering the case of a young woman we'll call Imani.

Imani's Story

Imani was raised by her maternal grandparents after her parents, who were battling drug addiction, abandoned her. Her grandparents were financially secure but were hoarders. In addition to living in crowded, unsanitary conditions, they hoarded their money. Imani knew her grandparents loved her, but they did not have the emotional well-being to care for a young child. As a result, many of Imani's needs were not met. She was often not permitted to eat enough for a growing child because her grandmother didn't want to spend too much money on food. Her grandmother took her to secondhand stores to buy clothes and made Imani choose items that were several sizes too big so she could grow into them. Imani felt as though she "looked like a clown" at school, and she struggled to fit in and make friends.

Every so often, Imani would spend time with her paternal grandparents, who were wealthy and lived a lavish lifestyle. While her everyday life was lonely and dreary, this alternate life seemed magical. This set of grandparents lived in a beautiful home, drove luxury cars, and wore designer clothes. They occasionally swooped into Imani's life and showered her with presents, vacations, and fancy meals at expensive restaurants. Then they plopped her back into her real life. Precious Imani, with her young, undeveloped brain, grappled to make sense of her challenging daily life and the fairytale life she occasionally experienced. Without healthy adult guidance, she concluded on her own that money equated to happiness. People with money, who wore nice clothes, lived in big houses, and went on glamorous vacations, were happy. People like her, who lived like paupers, were sad, friendless, and unworthy.

As Imani grew into adulthood, she became obsessed with image management. She was embarrassed by her grandparents, her home, her clothes, and her life. She got a job in high school so she could buy her own clothes, makeup, and hair products. She made every effort to be perceived by others as beautiful, successful, and likable. Since she never learned how to establish and maintain friendships appropriately, she believed her likability was based on how much she had to offer others.

Imani was repeatedly taken advantage of by friends and romantic partners because she allowed herself to be used. She frequently paid the entire bill when she went out for dinner with a group. She took her girlfriends shopping and treated them to pedicures to entice them to spend time with her. She did not honor her body in romantic relationships. She was sexual with men sooner than she wanted to be and agreed to sex acts she didn't want to participate in because she was so afraid of rejection if she said no. For Imani, nothing was worse than rejection. She was willing to do virtually anything to avoid being seen as unlovable.

By the time Imani went to therapy, her preoccupation with "looking perfect" was ruining her life. She spent so much time hyper-focusing on appearing "good enough" that she didn't have any idea who she was. Imani tried desperately to be likable and thought emulating the seemingly happy life of her wealthy grandparents would bring her the happiness she desired. However, despite her best efforts, she was as lonely and unhappy as ever. She believed she'd failed at life.

Stuck in her childlike way of thinking, Imani was convinced if she could just get the next big promotion, buy a new car, get a breast augmentation, wear the right shoes, or hang with a more successful crowd, then she might finally achieve happiness. Although this way of living failed her time and again, she was trapped believing she was unhappy because she had not yet reached a high enough status. She could not shift her thinking to realize the external things she obsessed over were never going to bring her happiness. The ongoing messaging encouraging her to "love herself" wasn't doing anything to help matters either.

It was hard for her to admit, but despite her best efforts, Imani hated herself. Worse, she came to hate all the people in her life she was constantly trying to impress. She wanted to be accepted by them, but she also saw them as superficial, unkind, and bad people whom she did not respect. Through the objective eyes of another, it was easy to understand why Imani felt so tormented. She was smart, beautiful, creative, talented, and kind. She was lovable in every way, but a childhood marked by abandonment and solitude left her riddled with insecurity and self-loathing.

Imani experienced a common psychological phenomenon. When a person endures a childhood of physical or emotional deprivation, they often grow into an adult who yearns for more and more, never feeling satiated. Imani yearned for love, belonging, friendship, acceptance, and validation. Unfortunately, because she felt so unworthy to her core, no amount of external affirmation could satisfy her needs.

Even with extensive therapy, it was initially difficult for Imani to see that her feelings of inadequacy were not based in reality but, rather, in painful childhood experiences. Her journey to wellness required her to go back in time and connect with the little girl she once was. When she reframed her self-doubt as fear brought up by that lonely little girl, she softened toward herself and responded to her insecurity with gentle kindness. It was the development of self-compassion that ultimately allowed Imani to shift the way she saw herself and her life.

In time, Imani learned to intervene on her distorted beliefs. When the thought "You'd better say yes or he won't like you" popped into her head, she recognized it as the voice of a scared, unhappy girl who was abandoned by her parents to live in disarray with mentally unfit grandparents. With practice and guidance, she learned to embrace that little girl with the compassion of a wise, understanding adult. She engaged in compassionate dialogue with herself to challenge her old belief systems.

Eventually, Imani started to see herself the way she truly was: a bright, thoughtful, funny, young woman who deserved better than the people in her early life gave her. She came to realize that if the adults in her life had done right by her, she would not have come to believe that she was unworthy and unlovable. In a different childhood, Imani might have grown to see herself as capable, worthy, and lovable, because that was the truth. This realization was unexpected and life-changing for Imani. She still struggled to feel worthy of self-love, but objectively she recognized that she was not inherently unworthy or unlovable. Her difficult childhood experiences imprinted lies onto her regarding herself, others, and the world, which made self-love extremely difficult for her despite her being a genuinely lovable person.

Over time, the intentional practice of self-compassion allowed Imani to see herself through a more empathic lens. She consistently challenged her unkind inner voice and, ultimately, became gentler and more understanding toward herself and others. Even though Imani couldn't feel the self-love she heard others talk about, she could see herself as naturally worthy and lovable in the same way other humans are born worthy and lovable.

Do you see how this is different from the "just love yourself" messaging we get from the media all the time? Imani found self-acceptance through self-compassion, and then she found self-neutrality through self-acceptance. She came to accept that being herself was enough, even when she was faced with uncomfortable situations and the judgments of others. She knew she didn't have to prove herself to others to earn their affection, even when those old voices crept in. Imani fought her urges to fall into old thinking patterns by reminding herself that she deserved the same respect everyone else does. She was able to see others as insecure humans just like her, which allowed her to be less harsh in her view of them as well. Learning to see herself and others in a more neutral way was a game changer in how Imani felt about herself and how she interacted with others. She described this transformation as freeing and said it allowed her to feel liberated from the neglect and abandonment she experienced as a child.

The Science of Self-Compassion

I'm going to introduce some self-compassion exercises to you in a moment, but I predict if you are like most of my self-loathing therapy clients, you're going to hate them—at first. You might even be annoyed at me for suggesting them to you. So, with that prediction in mind, I am first going to give you some information on the neuroscience of self-compassion and share some outcomes from research on self-compassion to hopefully win some credibility with you.

Here's the first thing you need to know: Both self-criticism and self-compassion are systems designed to keep us safe. However, self-criticism generates from the amygdala, which is a part of the brain that releases stress hormones, including cortisol and adrenaline. This activates our primal fight-flight-freeze response and prepares us to deal with a threat, which is great unless the threat is you, attacking yourself. In contrast, self-compassion is associated with a more advanced part of the brain known as the prefrontal cortex, which is responsible for higher-order thinking and problem-solving. This is a much wiser, more advanced part of the brain. So, to put it simply, self-criticism is far more instinctual because it's more primal, whereas self-compassion is far more effective because it's more advanced.

Think about it this way: You can use an early-model cell phone from 2007, or you can use one that came out this year. They will both allow you to make a call, but we all know which product is better. You don't want to use the "early-model" functions of your brain to solve the complex problems of the modern world. You have a far more advanced thinking center at your disposal for that.

Have I convinced you that self-compassion is smarter, more sophisticated, and more effective than self-criticism, even though it feels much less intuitive? Let me give you an example of how this plays out in the research. One study showed that people who talked to themselves like a good friend for seven days in a row lowered their depression levels for three months and raised their happiness levels for six months. If just one week of self-compassion has such dramatic effects on mental health, imagine what it could do for you if you practiced it for a few minutes every day!

Studies have also shown that self-compassion meditation can reduce pain among chronic pain sufferers. For example, in a study published by James Carson and colleagues in the *Journal of Holistic Nursing*, forty-three chronic back-pain sufferers participated in either an eight-week course on "the loving-kindness meditation" or received standard care for their back pain. Meditators had significantly less pain after eight weeks than those who received standard back pain care.

Another study out of Boston College examined people with chronic back pain who engaged in compassion toward others in a "patient-to-peer" program. Results showed that patients who helped other chronic pain sufferers significantly reduced their own pain. Compassion works, whether it's directed toward ourselves or others who suffer with the same afflictions we do. It's scientifically proven that compassion heals us.

Exercises in Self-Compassion

Now that you know I'm not just making up all this about the efficacy of self-compassion, let's explore some self-compassion practices you can integrate into your life. I'm going to give you several ideas, but you don't need to do them all. Choose one or two that you like (or don't hate too much) and try them out. Remember, it's going to feel weird, and you aren't going to see results right away. Be patient, be consistent, and you will eventually see results.

In my practice, when my clients are just starting to understand that the science really does back up the whole idea of self-compassion as a tool for healing, I move into the exercises by reminding them of their humanity. Humans are mammals, and all mammals are born very immature. They need warmth, connection, and love to feel safe. Humans are highly sensitive to physical touch, so you can calm yourself by placing your hand over your heart, giving yourself a neck massage, or giving yourself a butterfly hug (crossing your arms around your chest and squeezing the opposite arm). These are referred to as "bottom-up techniques" because you start by connecting with your body and allow your body to send signals up to your brain that it is safe to relax and feel at peace. And yes, the science backs this up too.

With this in mind, the next time you find yourself struggling, try placing your hand over your heart and saying, "I'm so sorry you (or we) are going through this. This is so hard. It's okay to just be sad and cry right now. Anyone in your position would feel this way." You don't have to use this script, but you get the idea. Say something kind, gentle, and validating to yourself and try to slip a little common humanity in there.

You can also try taking a "self-compassion break." Think of something in your life that causes you suffering and say to yourself, "This is a moment of suffering" or "This is really hard right now." Then connect to our common humanity with a statement like

"Suffering is a part of life" or "It's so human to feel this way." Finally, adopt a compassionate posture (for example, by placing your hand over your heart or giving yourself a hug) and say, "May I be kind to myself in this moment. May I give myself compassion and grace." If you need something even more neutral, try, "All humans feel pain and right now I feel pain. This is human, but it feels terrible. All human feelings are temporary, and I just need to get through this the best I can without making it worse."

In his book *I Heart Me*, Dr. David Hamilton offers four additional self-compassion strategies. As I've already predicted, you will probably be bad at this in the beginning. It will likely be challenging, and undoubtedly, your inner critic will tell you it's stupid and pointless. So again, just anticipate that and be ready to counter your self-criticism with a statement like "Okay, brain, I know you're trying to help, but you *haven't* been very helpful up to this point, so I'm going to try something different!" Then try one of the following four training exercises. They are all journaling exercises, so get yourself a journal if you don't have one already:

- Swap a self-defeating thought for a gentle one. For example, change "I'm a failure" to "I've had many successes." Then list some successes you've had so you can come back to them later.

- Make a list of your positive attributes (they don't have to be 100 percent true all the time). Include the things you are working on as well. While you're at it, make a list of ways you've been kind, compassionate, patient, and gentle with others.

- Create a list of times you coped with a challenge well, didn't make a bad situation worse, or showed courage in the face or fear.

- List some of your happiest moments. Then take a self-compassionate pose and hold for two minutes while you say affirming statements to yourself. You can imagine these words coming from an older, wiser version of you. Imagine this version of you as a friend rooting for your success, and take in the warm, loving messages they have for you.

Be Patient with Yourself

When a dear friend of mine (who is also a childhood trauma survivor) learned I was writing this book, she wrote to me, "PLEASE talk about how you are not hopeless and doomed just because doing affirmations in a mirror makes you want to punch yourself in the face!" That gives you a sense of how trauma survivors feel about this in the beginning. I had to smile when I reminded her that she is clearly benefiting from her self-compassion practice because she realizes that affirmations *do* work when you give them a real chance.

With that in mind, consider this: When you catch the harsh voice in your head trying to talk you out of self-compassion, ask yourself, "What would I say to someone I loved if they were struggling this way? What would I tell a friend who felt unworthy for the same reasons I do?" Most likely, you would offer loving, reassuring words.

Likewise, you can try saying kind, compassionate, or neutral statements to yourself. This is where you move from talking about self-neutrality in theory to putting it into practice. Here are some ideas:

- I am hurting.
- It's natural to feel this way.
- Everyone struggles sometimes, and I am only human.
- I commit to being kind and gentle to myself during this difficult period.
- It's okay to be disappointed.
- It's okay to be sad.
- I'm going to support myself through this.
- I am imperfect, just like everyone else, but I am doing my best.
- I'm working hard, even though this is difficult.
- I'm proud of myself.

For added benefit, say your self-compassion statements while engaging in a self-care activity, such as when you are taking a bath or meditating. Give yourself a neck and shoulder massage with an essential oil. Say your affirmations while taking a walk or during a yoga class. If you have a pet, cuddle with them and speak out loud to yourself in their voice. If I'm cuddling with my sweet goldendoodle, Meli, I might say, "You think I'm smart, don't you, Mel? Yes, you believe in me. I'm the most brilliant human you know!" I know, it's silly. But a little silliness can make me feel much lighter when things in my life are heavy.

My personal favorite skill is the loving-kindness meditation, which was done in the study I mentioned earlier by James Carson and colleagues. The loving-kindness meditation derives from Buddhism, and it's been the focus of many research experiments. It's a simple script you can follow, so you don't have to come up with any of your own words or ideas if you're struggling with that part. You can find versions of this meditation online, on YouTube, or on various meditation apps. It's well-known and easy to access. I'll give you a basic overview here.

First, sit with your body in a comfortable position. Feel free to take a self-compassionate pose. Close your eyes if that feels safe to you, but if it doesn't, just soften your gaze. Take a few long, slow breaths to connect inward, and then imagine the face of a person toward whom you have warm, loving feelings. It doesn't even need to be a person. It can be a pet or a loved one who has passed. It just needs to be someone you find very easy to love, preferably someone who makes you smile when you think of them. Now, as you imagine them in your mind's eye, offer them loving-kindness with the following phrases: "May you be happy. May you be safe. May you be healthy. May you be at peace."

Next, turn your attention toward yourself. You will now offer yourself the same loving-kindness you just gave to your loved one: "May I be happy. May I be safe. May I be healthy. May I be at peace." You may notice a big shift in how it feels to say that to yourself. If you have been struggling with self-criticism or self-hatred, you might even find it doesn't feel good to say these kind words to yourself. That's okay. It's expected early on, and it won't always feel like that.

Now, think of a person you know but with whom you have a neutral relationship. Maybe you see them around the office, but you don't know them well. Maybe it's a barista at your local coffee shop or a checkout person at your favorite grocery store. Offer them loving-kindness next: "May you be happy. May you be safe. May you be healthy. May you be at peace."

Next, think about a person you love but with whom you have a troubled relationship. Now offer this person loving-kindness: "May you be happy. May you be safe. May you be healthy. May you be at peace." This one might be hard. That's okay. Keep trying and give yourself some grace and compassion as you practice.

Finally, you can think of all humanity, everyone, everywhere, sharing this human experience with you. Everyone is doing their best to make it through life while experiencing joy, insecurity, sorrow, and every other human emotion. Extend loving-kindness to all of humanity at the same time, yourself included: "May we be happy. May we be safe. May we be healthy. May we be at peace."

You will probably feel different emotions during each phase of the meditation. Some parts may feel good, and others may bring about distress. This is normal. Try not to judge yourself at all and just be curious about the observations you make. Over time, this practice will help you develop a sense of true self-worth. No clichés, no gimmicks. It's the foundation you need for getting to a place of self-neutrality, a place of peace and acceptance.

Take the time to build your tolerance for self-kindness and compassion. You must become a dear friend to yourself. Think about your favorite people. Do you believe they are worthy and deserving of compassion, care, and respect? I imagine you do. Are they only worthy and deserving because they are infallible? Of course not. Do you love and accept them only because they are perfect? Okay, you get where I'm going here. You love and accept your friends despite their flaws. You believe they are worthy and deserve happiness even in their state of imperfection. Ultimately, you must develop this kind, accepting relationship with yourself. The work you do to get there will be well worth it.

CHAPTER 6

How Social Media Impacts Mental Health

It's time to talk about the big elephant in the room. Or, rather, the phone. And that elephant is social media. I have no doubt that even the mention of social media has some of you reading this having a visceral reaction. Maybe you love social media and can't imagine your life without it. Maybe you hate it, and just the thought of downloading Instagram, Facebook, or TikTok gives you anxiety. No matter where you fall on the spectrum, it's important that you read this chapter with an open mind.

Let me start by saying I think social media has been a huge ally to the mental health field in many ways. I don't think any other platform in history has helped communities talk about mental health, destigmatize negative attitudes about therapy, or encourage people of marginalized communities to come together and advocate the way social media has. To its credit, the internet has made mental health treatment more accepted and accessible all over the world.

That's the good news.

Now for the bad news. There are other ways in which social media has created negative mental health outcomes and spread dangerously high levels of misinformation about mental health all over the internet. I think it's important for everyone to be cognizant of the information they consume and be intentional about what they allow themselves to take in. The bottom line is that whether you consume information from the news, television and movies, podcasts, or the YouTubers and influencers you follow, this information can either be helpful or harmful to your mental and emotional well-being. This is especially true when you consider how much influence the internet has on how we feel about ourselves in comparison to how we perceive others.

I'm probably not telling you anything you haven't heard before. And yet I find that it bears repeating. Social media is an amazing resource but should be used with an abundance of caution. That is especially true if you are suffering from the impact of childhood trauma that has negatively affected how you view yourself.

To make matters more complicated, the social-media landscape changes at breakneck speed. For example, I have an Instagram account, @drheidigreen, where I provide mental health information and education. Most of it is specific to trauma healing because it's so important for mental health experts to play a role in providing accurate information to the masses and dispelling the multitudes of inaccurate information flying around. As a young Gen-Xer, I received my clinical training in the early 2000s, when social media existed but also when it was considered a big ethical no-no to have any kind of online presence as a mental health expert.

Back then, psychology students were told to make all our social media pages private (or better yet, not to have any at all). We were constantly warned of all the possible conflicts of interest, breaches of confidentiality, and potential board complaints we would open ourselves up to if our clients found us on social media. "Protect yourself and your business at all costs" was the takeaway message.

The idea that the public might see us as human beings who go on vacations, have spouses and children, or have opinions about things outside the realm of mental health was seen as a threat to both our personal and professional safety. Don't get your professor started on what might happen if people accessed pictures of you on social media going to happy hours, going on dates, or being dolled up in a slinky dress killing it in a karaoke bar! One of my professors told our class that no matter where we were or what we were doing, we were always representing psychology and ourselves as psychologists.

I agreed at the time, but as my cohort and I transitioned from students to early-career psychologists, we believed more and more there was a world of good we could do if we presented ourselves as relatable people and used the internet to advocate for mental health awareness. We also saw other people in our field showing more and more of their authentic selves online and saw that it wasn't all terrible. In fact, they might have been doing some good for their clients by being "real" people with their own struggles, lives, and need for connection and acceptance.

We didn't know what to expect, or how it would go at the time, but I am so pleased mental health practitioners forged into the world of social media. I believe making ourselves more accessible to the community and to potential therapy consumers has been good for the field of psychology and for the public more broadly. There are a lot of incredibly talented therapists on Facebook, Instagram, TikTok, and YouTube who are all putting out wonderful content. People who can't afford therapy or who don't have easy access to quality therapists in their area can access free posts, videos, and blogs, as well as inexpensive books and courses, on an array of mental health topics via social media.

And yet, while all that is fabulous, there is a flip side.

The Downside of Mental Health in Social Media

The rise of mental health information on the internet has also led to the rise of misinformation. It has created several problems for people living with mental health conditions and for members of vulnerable communities. For example, there was a time when therapists introduced psychological terminology to their clients in a therapy session. These therapists explained psychological phenomena to their clients in a way that was custom-tailored to them, including how the terms directly impacted their lives. Today, clinical terms are shared with the public by nonexperts—out of context—and people enthusiastically misuse their newfound terminology.

We now live in an online world where anyone can believe they are "educated" enough to diagnose themselves and others with mental health conditions. Terms that have clinical meaning like narcissistic personality disorder, gaslighting, borderline personality disorder, abuse, and even the words *trauma* and *triggers* are being used wildly out of context. Our clinical terms are being diluted and losing their meaning and, in many cases, are being used as weapons to hurt and manipulate others. This contributes to less safety for people living with mental health conditions and more situations in which trauma and abuse survivors aren't believed and fail to get necessary services.

Here's an example. I see people on social media throwing the words *narcissist* and *narcissistic abuse* out like candy. These are hot, trendy terms that should be reserved for people who meet criteria for narcissistic personality disorder and for the victims of their abuse. Narcissistic abuse often qualifies as domestic violence, and victims frequently need support getting out of the relationship and reestablishing safety in their lives.

When people claim that every a-hole they dated is a narcissist, and every person who lies or cheats is a narcissistic abuser, these terms lose their clinical value. This terminology has been thrown around so frequently that many people now roll their eyes anytime they hear the word *narcissist*. This has created a huge problem for those who are trapped in relationships where intimate partner violence is happening at the hands of someone who truly does have a personality disorder. When these victims speak out and ask for help, there's now a higher chance that they won't be taken seriously or get access to necessary safety resources in a timely matter. This is dangerous for victims of abuse and domestic violence.

I am increasingly frustrated with the misuse of words like *trauma* and *triggered* as well. I have heard many people say on social media that "no one gets to define what is traumatic for you" and "you get to decide what is trauma and what isn't." Though many will agree, I take issue with this because while it is true that all people react to trauma differently, we can't allow for anything and everything to be defined as trauma. We know potentially traumatic events may or may not become locked into a person's body based on how they processed the events at the time and what kind of resources they had to help them. But we must be realistic about what we call trauma. I see many people on the internet describing themselves as "traumatized" when dealing with typical human challenges we all face.

Why do I bring this up? Because speaking with precision is incredibly important when it comes to moving into self-acceptance, self-compassion, and ultimately self-neutrality. Words are powerful. And as you know already, how you speak to yourself is powerful. All the more reason to understand the impact, both positive and negative, of the rise of "therapy speak" on social media.

If you're a person living with the very real effects of trauma, abuse, or complex trauma, it might be offensive to you to read someone say they were "traumatized" after a disagreement with a friend or "triggered" by a rude server in a restaurant. You may feel incredibly dismissed when you read someone's post about the "trauma" they went through after having a rough day at work. You might worry that if these typical human experiences are considered traumatic, then the experiences you've endured on a much greater scale make you even more "different from" or "less than" others. This might perpetuate your belief that you aren't "normal," are "too much," or are permanently damaged. You might fear that you'll never find real connection with others because they will never know or understand you the way you long to feel known and understood.

Let me add a disclaimer here, because when I post on Instagram suggesting it's not appropriate to call every unpleasant experience trauma, some people get very upset with me. I obviously cannot speak to the experiences of every person on earth in an Instagram post or even in this book. If you thought, "Well, I had a disagreement with a friend that *was* traumatizing because that friend was an abusive person and I had to cut off contact to protect myself," then my comment wasn't meant for you. If you thought, "I had a really abusive boss and I felt emotionally beaten down every day for a year when I worked for them," again, my comment wasn't about you or about situations like yours.

One of my primary concerns about social media is how reactive, defensive, and argumentative people have become with each other. I am perplexed by the number of people who are fired up and ready to argue about topics they know little about with experts who have dedicated their lives to mastering the subject (scientists everywhere are nodding along here). My point is, it's easy to misconstrue written text and even easier to fire off in anger toward a stranger on the internet in a way you never would do to a person standing right in front of you. And you can imagine what all that reactivity and anger is doing to your ability to see things from a neutral perspective.

Simply put, social media has contributed to so many advances in mental health awareness, but it has also made people more reactive, more likely to see themselves as experts on complex topics they have only a basic understanding of, and far more likely to pop off and behave with rage and ugliness toward people they don't know. It's my opinion that many people come to social media to find validation for their unhealthy beliefs and dysfunctional behaviors, instead of coming with an open mind or a desire to grow into a better version of themselves.

As a therapist, part of my job is to disrupt unhelpful thought patterns, and sometimes that makes people upset. We can't make progress without getting uncomfortable and facing the darker parts of ourselves.

The bottom line is, millions of fallible humans interact with each other every day on social media, making it a breeding ground for misinformation, fragile egos, and dysfunctional (and sometimes unhinged) behavior. With so much chaos and so many opinions being presented as facts, it's easy to see why many people believe and spread false information. As a trauma survivor and mental health professional, I will keep unapologetically calling it out when I see it. And as a trauma survivor yourself, you need to be extra careful about how you consume and interact with online information.

A Healthy Online Community

Let's shift now to the comparison game on social media that causes so many people to feel inferior. Most of us are already aware that people, especially influencers, present their best selves online. And unfortunately, we subconsciously compare their *best* to our *worst*. We know that influencers are curating, photoshopping, and filtering to create a facade of perfection. We then compare that facade to all our many imperfections. It's difficult not to feel jealous of people who are more fit, seem more attractive, dress better, go on amazing vacations, have high-paying powerful jobs, or just present their lives as unrealistically happy and ideal.

Remember, influencers make their livings by convincing you that they have it all figured out and that if you want to be as happy, successful, beautiful, and worthy as they are, you need to follow them, click on their links, buy their products, or take their courses. The money they make off *your* insecurities supports their livelihood. People who are already insecure, self-doubting, struggling with self-worth, and beating themselves up over not being "good enough" are easy prey for the superficial world of social media influencers. As a clinician, I must admit that the psychology of it all is quite sophisticated.

Let me add here that I'm obviously not talking about every influencer on the internet. I don't know every influencer! I also know many influencers *are* putting out helpful content and doing good in the world on their platforms (heck, I consider myself one of those people!). I'm speaking of a particular type of influencer, the type who might be offering "just love yourself" platitudes that garner lots of likes and contain little substance.

Let's look at this in a neutral way. A lot of people use their social media accounts to receive the validation that all humans need. It's natural to want to present all the best parts of our lives and not broadcast all our struggles. As pack animals, being well-liked and accepted is imperative to our survival. We need to be connected to other people, and for those who struggle to find in-person human connection, the sense of connection and validation we get through social media might be the best option we have. I don't mean to put down anyone for how they use social media. I do want us all to understand how it can hurt us if we aren't mindful about how we use it.

When Dr. Neff writes about self-compassion, she explains how self-compassion is an act of loving and accepting yourself *despite* your failures and weaknesses. This is why it's so important to be intentional about what you consume. Are you following people who make you feel good (or at least neutral)? Do they bring you hope or make you feel better about humanity and maybe even better about yourself? Or do you follow people who make you feel insecure, incapable, undeserving, or even self-loathing?

It's common for people who already feel bad about themselves to seek confirmation that they're as defective as they think they are. It's a part of confirmation bias therapists refer to as "pain-seeking." Although it seems to defy what we know about the brain's number one goal of keeping us safe, the traumatized brain has a warped sense of safety. Your traumatized brain can turn on you when it doesn't know how to fix a problem, and it thinks the only option is for you to stop being such a loser and go fix yourself. You may initially go to social media to find information that might help you improve your life, but because of confirmation bias, you can easily fall into the trap of overfocusing on what makes you feel bad and end up in a spiral of shame and despair.

As trauma survivors, we must not allow ourselves to fall into these traps. We must remember that the rules of common humanity apply to us. In my own healing journey, I needed to accept myself despite my childhood abuse, my shortcomings as a parent, my failed marriages, my anxiety, my self-doubt, and my hundreds of imperfections. It was easy to focus on how much I screwed things up. It was difficult to accept that I was still worthy of love, kindness, community, and compassion. It was even more difficult to accept that I needed to give those gifts to myself. Eventually, I did, and today I believe if we can't find some level of self-acceptance we can't fully make peace with our traumatic pasts.

Despite our desire to "pain-seek," we must continue to practice consuming information that encourages our brains to focus more on what's good in the world and less on how defective we feel. The brain builds itself based on what we feed it, so if you've been feeding it social comparison, jealousy, judgment, and negative self-talk, it's time to start feeding it something else.

I've heard all the arguments against this. *I'm not being hard on myself; I'm just being realistic. The world is full of horrible things; I can't just ignore the truth. I'm just tricking myself if I consume content that tries to make me feel good about myself. There's no point in seeking out feel-good content because I'm never going to believe it.* Believe me, I know it's difficult to get out of this type of thinking. I'm asking you to stretch yourself in a way that makes you uncomfortable and challenges your view of yourself, others, and the world.

Remember, most trauma survivors feel the way you do. No matter how much you hate yourself right now, you are not an exception to humanity. On the contrary, it's normal to feel this way after experiencing complex trauma. You don't need to change who you are. You just need to shift how you respond to yourself when your traumatized brain is in the driver's seat. Adjusting your relationship with social media might be a good place to start.

I can't tell you how many times I told myself what a worthless piece of shit I was over the years. How the world would be better off without me. How I should just end myself because I was a garbage person who destroyed everything I touched. That I was an idiot to think I deserved any amount of love or happiness. That I would never get it anyway, or if I did, it would only be to fool me into thinking I could be happy, and then it would be ripped away, and the universe would laugh at how stupid I was to have hoped for anything good.

I'm telling you, I've seen it all. I've heard it all. I've been there myself and I've felt it too. I was sure I was the exception, and no one would convince me otherwise. But I was wrong. I wasn't the exception, and you aren't either. But you will never see the truth about yourself if you don't start being mindful of the messages you are consuming and their impact on your ability to practice self-compassion.

Purging the social media content you consume that reinforces all the shitty things you say to yourself might be a good place to start. Cut back on your scrolling time and follow more therapists. Follow cute animal accounts. Follow comedians, activists, and people who are trying to make the world a better place. Stop filling your mind with garbage, and I promise, in time, you will start to feel less like garbage yourself. Or at the very least, start believing you deserve to be happy and healed from your past.

CHAPTER 7

Debunking the Myths of Pop Psychology

Let's begin with the obvious question: What is pop psychology? At its core, pop psychology is an oversimplification of psychological terms and practices that is often not rooted in scientific research. Pop psychology is a phenomenon that has become widespread thanks to the internet and especially social media. It's often presented as "fun," "lighthearted," and "feel-good" psychology that usually has a strong focus on self-help. While that certainly can be helpful, it can also make bankers, office managers, kindergarten teachers, and people of any profession think they are mental health experts even when they are not.

The "personality" quiz you took online to find out what breed of dog you are? Pop psychology. That "mental health hack" you heard about on TikTok? Pop psychology. All those quick fixes to difficult psychological issues you read about? You guessed it, pop psychology. These concepts are quite popular, and we find them everywhere, even in best-selling books. For example, the book *Men Are from Mars, Women Are from Venus*, which has been criticized for oversimplifying complex human dynamics and romantic relationships, was written by a self-proclaimed personal relationship counselor who had no mental health degrees or certifications.

Perhaps most concerning about pop psychology is its strong emphasis on personal feelings, which can cause us to over-pathologize (exaggerate) typical human experiences. It's important to listen to our emotions and use them in tandem with our logic to make good decisions and accurate assessments about our surroundings. However, when we overfocus on our feelings, we risk falling into self-pity, victimization, blame, and a lack of personal responsibility. My experience of complex trauma survivors is that they often present with the opposite of this problem. They can be incredibly self-blaming—finding themselves responsible for all kinds of things that couldn't possibly have been their fault—and rather than engage in self-pity, they are often more self-shaming.

If you're struggling with any of these issues, I don't want to send the wrong message. Instead, I want to make you aware that people who have not experienced trauma on the scale you have might present themselves as "traumatized," "victimized," "abused," and "triggered" when those terms really don't apply to them. When you read their claims, it might make you feel angry or dismissed, and that's valid.

Speaking of validating feelings, pop psychology has made way for a generation of young people who believe all their feelings should be "validated" and all their wants and needs should be "normalized." Again, some of this has had a positive impact. The idea of normalizing therapy and normalizing mental health days are great examples of how the "let's normalize it" culture has improved our understanding of mental health. But the online obsession with believing you should be validated all the time has caused a lot of problems.

Not every feeling needs to be validated. Not every feeling *should* be validated. It may be a fact that you feel a certain way, and there may be a very logical reason you're experiencing that emotion, but it doesn't necessarily mean it's the most appropriate emotion for the situation. It could be an inappropriate or exaggerated response to the situation.

Let me give you an example of what I mean. When a smoke detector in our house sounds the alarm, we don't start screaming "FIRE!" We don't run out of the house and immediately call 911. The smoke alarm goes off to let us know there is a situation to investigate. We might get a little nervous, but we are probably going to head into the kitchen to see what's going on. Most of the time, it's something minor. Maybe we burned cookies in the oven or bread in the toaster. Generally, it's a situation we can take care of ourselves.

The brain also acts like a smoke alarm. It alerts us to situations that might be problematic so we can investigate and determine if something needs our attention. Unfortunately, this smoke detector sometimes malfunctions, and the alarm keeps sounding even when smoke isn't present. This can cause us to have an overreaction or a misinformed reaction. In these cases, the simple platitudes of pop psychology can make things worse by "validating" our misguided ideas instead of challenging them.

This is in contrast to what happens in the therapy room. When a client struggles with trauma responses out in the world, I provide them with psychoeducation, which is education on psychological research or any other empirically validated information that can help them understand what's going on inside them.

For example, I may teach them that the amygdala, which is the brain's stress response center, releases cortisol whenever it encounters a situation that reminds it of a previous traumatic experience. I explain that, when this happens, the amygdala asks the hippocampus (the brain's memory center), "Hey, is everything okay? What's going on?" In a traumatized brain, the hippocampus may not be able to assess the situation properly, so it tells the amygdala, "Danger ahead! Get ready!" In turn, the amygdala dumps stress hormones into the blood stream to activate the fight-flight-freeze response. Unfortunately, if the hippocampus has misinterpreted the situation, that hormone release is going to create about twenty to sixty minutes of physical and emotional activation that isn't necessary.

If this happens during a disagreement with a romantic partner, we may begin yelling, name-calling, blaming, making accusations, assuming malintent where there is none, or even making threats. We feel validated in our exaggerated response because we believed the misinformation we received from the hippocampus, and the amygdala overreacted accordingly. In cases like this, we don't deserve the validation we desire because our belief was inaccurate, and our response was inappropriate.

Hopefully, you can see how important this is to understand. When pop psychology says, "always trust your gut" and "all your feelings are valid," it fails to recognize the highly nuanced circumstances we face as unique individuals. You may insist that someone validate you, apologize, or even "admit the truth" when your "gut" perception of the situation is wrong. It isn't fair to insist that others agree you deserve validation, because sometimes you don't. In fact, sometimes you respond so poorly to something that your behavior overshadows the issue that made you upset in the first place. You allow yourself to become so offensive in your emotional state that the person who needs to reflect and apologize is *you*.

Maybe there was a good reason you felt the way you did. It may be completely logical that you thought your partner lied to you if they spoke to you in a way that reminded you of how your ex used to lie to you. But just because your response is *understandable* doesn't make it correct or valid. This is where all that oversimplified pop psychology can make you more dysfunctional, not less.

I can't tell you how many times I've watched online arguments about topics like this unfold on social media. Therapists get verbally attacked by people who have only superficial understanding of a topic thanks to what pop psychology told them. They are determined to stick with this incomplete version of things because it confirms what they already want to believe. They may have some information they believe is "scientific" and allow themselves to act out against others and feel justified. They also may be unwilling to hear actual science that refutes their belief. It's understandable, but it isn't healthy. In this way, pop psychology makes our society sicker, more immature, and less accountable.

I've mentioned confirmation bias a few times already, so allow me to explain how pop psychology intersects with confirmation bias and causes all kinds of societal problems. In case you're not sure what I'm talking about, confirmation bias is the human tendency to seek out information that agrees with or validates the opinions and beliefs we already hold.

If I believe the earth is round, I can find lots of scientific evidence and research online to confirm my belief. But if I think the earth is flat, I can type "proof the earth is flat" into a search engine and find lots of articles and websites that will support this belief too. Humans don't always do a great job genuinely educating themselves and will sift through "fake news" and "pseudoscience" to find their desired answers. Sometimes people just want to find "proof" of their preconceived notions so they can use that information to argue with others who disagree with them.

How many times have you been watching a thread where people fight among each other and post random articles, websites, or news stories (no matter how bizarre the source is)? Thanks to the internet, if you want to believe something, you can find confirming material in a matter of seconds. So, let's bust some pop psychology myths pertaining to this book, shall we?

MYTH #1: You can't love anyone else until you love yourself.

Truth: You are capable of love as all humans are capable of love. You are worthy of love right now, just as you are, even if you don't believe it. That said, if you believe you're unlovable, it will certainly cause some attachment disruptions or show up in the way you perceive your loved ones' actions. It will probably impact how you react to them in times of stress (or even in good times, because you're always waiting for the other shoe to drop). If you want to have happy, healthy, fulfilling relationships with others, you will have to stop hating yourself. You don't have to *love* yourself, but you at least need to accept yourself and be *neutral* toward yourself so that your self-loathing doesn't bleed into all your interpersonal relationships.

MYTH #2: If someone argues with you or lies to you, they are gaslighting you.

Truth: *Gaslighting* is one of those terms that gets horribly misused on the internet. Gaslighting is not the same as disagreeing, and it is not synonymous with lying. Everyone lies, not everyone gaslights.

Gaslighting is an abusive behavior in which an individual knows the truth (and they know *you* know the truth), but they attempt to convince you that you're crazy by insisting the thing you know is true absolutely did not happen. Here's an example: My partner tells me to change my outfit before we leave for an event because my dress "makes me look fat." I feel embarrassed and shocked, but I don't question it, I just change. Later in the evening after we get home, I confront him and say, "It really hurt my feelings when you said I looked fat and insisted I change." He responds, "I never said that! You asked if you looked fat, and I said if you felt uncomfortable in that outfit, you should just change."

In this case, my partner is "crazy making" by insisting the conversation we just had a few hours ago didn't happen. He accuses *me* of saying the hurtful thing he said and is attempting to make himself look like a supportive boyfriend when he purposefully tried to make me feel bad about myself.

He doubles down every time I insist he acknowledge the truth. He repeatedly attempts to convince me I misunderstood the whole thing, and he might even say things like "You're crazy, I would never say that" or "I can't believe you would accuse me of saying such a hurtful thing." He makes himself the victim and tries to get me to question my reality and, if possible, feel bad enough to apologize to him.

The goal of his gaslighting is to make me believe I cannot trust myself and trick me into thinking I need him to tell me what is real and what isn't. It's a long con, a pattern of manipulation with a sinister end goal, and it isn't just a one-off argument or untruth. It's a malicious attempt to make me doubt myself and depend on him. This malicious *intention* makes all the difference in gaslighting. That's what makes it emotional abuse.

MYTH #3: Happiness is a choice.

Truth: I honestly can't think of anything more offensive or dismissive than to tell a person who is suffering that happiness is a choice. Toxic positivity is rampant on social media, just another oversimplified solution to a complex problem. It's so easy for people who aren't trauma survivors to say, "Look at the bright side. Think of all your many blessings!" How lovely it must be to live without mental illness, but for those of us who do, telling us, "It could be worse" or "Just focus on the positive" feels like asking us to breathe water or swim in air. It's incredibly invalidating and unrelatable, and if you are nodding along right now, I'm sorry you've experienced the dismissiveness of well-meaning but ignorant people.

Of course, you can't just "choose happiness." If it were a simple choice, you obviously would have already done it. I know you want to experience happiness and live in a state of peace. You deserve it, and I intend to set you on the path to find it, but there is absolutely nothing wrong with you if your traumatic past (or present) makes happiness feel impossible right now.

MYTH #4: You MUST learn to love yourself.

Truth: Social media is absolutely riddled with the message that self-love is a necessity in life. Admittedly, when I started my Instagram account many years ago, it was completely focused on self-love. I was still worried about all those warnings from my professors about participating in the social media realm and thought my best bet was to stay on a "safe" topic. I also knew how much trauma *does* impact a person's ability to love themselves. Eventually, my focus shifted to fostering self-love after trauma, and that was the inspiration for my first book.

Many trauma survivors are capable of self-love, and you might be too, even if it seems impossible now. As I have continued to learn and grow as a psychologist, and as the field of psychology has continued to evolve and improve as well, myself and other trauma therapists have become more and more aware that self-love isn't always possible, nor is it necessary for a content and fulfilling life.

Early on, many therapists started referring to "self-like" as an alternative to self-love. As we continue to understand trauma survivors more deeply, many of us are coming to see that a state of self-positivity is not the only answer. Self-acceptance, self-kindness, self-compassion, and ultimately self-neutrality are the most attainable options for many childhood and complex trauma survivors, and it's not just a consolation prize. It's a satisfying, healing, and very realistic option.

MYTH #5: Arguing is emotional abuse.

Truth: Conflict with others is a normal part of the human experience. Being angry, annoyed, disappointed, frustrated, hurt, or shocked by the behaviors of people we love is typical and expected. Sometimes we overreact, say things we don't mean, and must apologize and make things right with the people we love. Over-pathologizing these normal human experiences is not healthy or appropriate. When we do this, we unnecessarily put ourselves in a victim position and give away both our power and our personal responsibility.

I'm going to be blunt here—throwing around the word *abuse* to gain sympathy and avoid accountability for your part in your dysfunctional relationships is childish. This is one of those cases where "normalizing" something creates more harm than good. Anecdotally, I have found that trauma and abuse survivors often understand and agree with this sentiment on social media, whereas people who exaggerate these terms for their benefit tend to be the ones who get most defensive and reactive to my posts on this subject.

MYTH #6: All my feelings are valid and deserve to be validated by others.

Truth: We've discussed this at length already, but let's just examine the lack of logic here. If all feelings are valid, and all *your* feelings are valid, then everyone else's feelings are also valid, right? Whomever you disagree with also has valid feelings and you need to acknowledge them. Their outburst toward you is just as valid as your outburst toward them, so no one is ever accountable for their bad behavior because everyone should be validated all the time. This is silly. To assume all your feelings and reactions are always valid is to assume that anyone who thinks or feels differently than you is invalid. We all need to be mature adults, examine our behavior, and be willing to acknowledge when our feelings or behaviors are *understandable* based on our past experiences, but are not *valid* based on the present situation.

MYTH #7: My partner was "grooming" or "love bombing" me in the beginning of our relationship to manipulate me into believing they were someone other than who they really are.

Truth: Maybe? But maybe not. Everyone who has hurt you is not a narcissist. Everyone who betrays you isn't an abuser. Sometimes people just do shitty things because they are imperfect humans. We all treat people badly sometimes. Often, we regret it later. I certainly behaved terribly in some of my early adulthood relationships and would never want my entire existence to be defined by what an ex has to say about the time we spent together long ago.

We all want grace for ourselves when we aren't our best, and we need to extend that grace to others. Someone may have had genuine feelings of love and warmth for you at one point, and sometimes that fades, and they don't handle it well. When we label all people who hurt us as "narcissists" and "abusers," we minimize the experiences of trauma and abuse survivors. Our experiences hold weight, and that heaviness deserves to be honored, not trivialized by those seeking attention and validation.

I wish we could go back to a time when we used adjectives, not labels, to describe our experiences with certain people and that we could leave the psychology jargon and the diagnosing of mental health conditions to the people who are qualified to do it. This might resonate for you, and you may have had repeated experiences with people who ignorantly dismissed your abuse by comparing it to their typical human conflicts or common unpleasant experiences. It's likely an unfortunate side effect of psychological terms getting "normalized" into the culture through social media. Trauma-informed therapists call it out on their platforms and advocate for trauma survivors to be honored, but we only have so much power. This is our shared reality in the world of social media, so my best advice is for you to accept it's going to happen and protect yourself as much as you can from it.

MYTH #8: If you don't hate the same people I hate, or validate my hateful attitudes, you are dismissing my lived experience. In fact, you might be a bigot.

Truth: This idea that "I must always be validated" is bleeding into complex social and political issues and is being used as a weapon against people who aren't perfectly aligned with our own ideologies.

It is socially responsible to *not* develop strong opinions and rigid attitudes about complex conflicts we don't entirely understand and that don't impact us directly. There are lots of emotions and different worldviews that are all playing out at the same time everywhere on earth. So many different types of people are on social media advocating for their positions and their voices to be heard. It's a good thing. But it becomes toxic and damages our mental health when we use social media to disparage groups that are different from us, and shame people who won't hate alongside us. Worse, it keeps us isolated in feelings of love/hate, right/wrong, with me/against me, which makes it impossible to adopt a healthy sense of neutrality.

People who choose to express kindness and empathy for individuals on both sides of political and cultural disputes are called horrible names by extremists who insist that the only way to support their lived experience is to denounce someone else's. It can be such a challenge to stay neutral or acknowledge that two opposing groups might both have valid concerns. If you find that engaging in these online conversations makes you feel disheartened about the world or down about yourself, please reconsider your participation in these forums.

As trauma survivors, we may be more sensitive when exposed to stories of war, genocide, political unrest, sexual violence, and all forms of human suffering than people who are not trauma survivors. The human brain is not meant to absorb and process all the information about all the terrible things happening everywhere in the world. Our brains are still primitive in many ways, and we're only meant to know about the bad things happening in our own communities because we have some power to impact the things that happen in our immediate vicinity. The brain hates ambiguity and uncertainty, and nothing feels worse than being helpless and out of control. Many of us feel it's important to be informed about what is happening across the globe, and that's fine and appropriate. However, I caution you to be mindful about what and how much you consume so you don't harm yourself through overexposure to atrocities far away that you have no power to improve.

MYTH #9: You just need more self-care!

Truth: Yes, self-care is important. We all need and deserve self-care. But self-care alone has never healed anyone's complex trauma. It's a helpful practice and one part of a big project when it comes to trauma healing, but telling someone they "just need more self-care" is yet another example of how toxic positivity and superficial solutions are harmful to those who are carrying the burden of complex trauma.

It can be frustrating when people throw out silly antidotes at you, like "Nature is my therapy!" or "Sunshine is medicine!" While there's a little truth to these statements, they are so oversimplified that they hold absolutely no weight when presented to a person processing years of trauma and abuse. Please know that it's okay to tell people you aren't interested in hearing their ideas about your mental health treatment. You can tell them you are working with a professional and following the healing plan you've built together.

It's also okay to set boundaries, like "It makes me uncomfortable to talk to others about my mental health. I know you want to help, but I must ask you to refrain from bringing up this topic again. I don't want to talk about it." A boundary can be the best way to respond to people who give you unsolicited advice when they clearly don't know what they are talking about.

MYTH #10: You just need to heal your inner child.

Truth: Listen, I do inner child work in my practice with survivors of childhood trauma. I introduce it if it's apparent my client will benefit from it, and only when they are emotionally ready to do it. "Inner child work" isn't a therapeutic modality. Rather, it's a concept stemming from many different types of therapeutic models. If you are a trauma survivor, it's best to do this work with a skilled trauma therapist.

The problem with doing exercises to connect to your inner child is that it doesn't make any sense to even try when you *hate* your inner child. Suggesting someone do it before they are ready is potentially damaging. Sure, there are some therapists on social media who suggest you can do it on your own. Some have developed online programs you can purchase to "self-heal." That might work for some people, but I can assure you there is a lot of healing work that goes on in a trauma therapy session that would be reckless to try on your own without the support of a skilled professional. Just because someone tells you they followed a psychologist's online program—or they read the psychologist's book and did the inner child or "shadow work" suggested in the program—does not mean it works for everyone and does not mean it's right for you.

The bottom line is, you absolutely don't need to subscribe to a certain method or follow anyone else's cookie-cutter plan for emotional well-being and mental health. You are a unique individual, and you know yourself better than anyone else ever will, including your therapist. You deserve a bespoke healing journey that is created *for* you and *with* you using evidence-based treatment models specific to trauma healing. No one else has the answer for you. As mental health professionals, our job is not to heal you, but to understand you, hold space for you, and guide you onto the right path for your healing based on your personal experiences and needs.

Healthy Engagement with Social Media

Let's tie everything together now. While pop psychology can be helpful for a large general audience, it fails to recognize the nuance of human experiences. For those who have lived through complex childhood trauma, these antidotes can not only be unhelpful, but also harmful, to recovery. The explosion of mental health information on social media has been phenomenal for breaking mental health stigma and normalizing therapy, and as a mental health expert, I'm thrilled. I also recognize it has created an environment in which misinformation is everywhere, and complex topics get whittled down to flashy memes and trite "inspirational" quotes that trauma survivors can find unrelatable and damaging.

On a positive note, people living with complex trauma often experience social media as a place to find others who can relate to their struggles and provide them with ideas for healing their long-standing wounds. Connecting with those who share our lived experiences can help us develop compassion for ourselves through compassion for others. When we are kind to those who have had similar traumatic experiences, it can make it easier for us to be kind to ourselves.

We all desire answers that are simple enough to understand but profound enough to change our lives. Since terms like *self-love*, *body positivity*, *self-care*, *inner child healing*, and *shadow work* can be completely unrelatable for complex trauma survivors, leading them to feel even more isolated and broken, we need to be mindful and intentional about what we consume online. If you choose to use social media as a way to find mental health information or connect with others who share your lived experience, I suggest the following:

- Exercise critical thinking with all content you consume.
- Don't believe everything you read, no matter how cute the graphics.
- Don't follow accounts that make you feel bad about yourself.
- Be open to scientific evidence that transcends and challenges pop psychology.
- Stay coachable so you can take advantage of all the evidence-based knowledge experts share, even if they challenge your current belief systems.

Perhaps most important of all, remember the limitations of social media. Not every post is for you! If you don't agree with something, feel free to roll your eyes and scroll past it without joining into an argument that will likely just feed into your emotional disruption and deepen your overall negative view of people and the world.

I want to end this chapter on a positive note. It *is* possible to balance the benefits of social media with the need to think critically about the content you are creating and consuming. It's possible by practicing neutrality. It is downright liberating for someone who has suffered trauma to see others as fallible, and it's an amazing feeling to be able to scroll past a post instead of having a knee-jerk reaction. Give yourself the gift of being calm and neutral when scrolling online, maybe even open to what's being said. That way, you can be intentional about how you react—and decide whether the content is deserving of a reaction at all.

CHAPTER 8

Stop Gaslighting Yourself

I know, I know. In the previous chapter, I said people are overusing and misusing the word *gaslighting* to describe anyone who has treated them poorly, and now I have a chapter about how to stop gaslighting yourself. You're probably wondering how it is even *possible* to gaslight yourself.

Admittedly, since the word is so pervasive in pop psychology, I'm going to take some liberties with the term in this chapter. I'm doing that because it's the best way to phrase some of the toxic thought patterns complex trauma survivors find themselves in. Many trauma survivors take on the voice of their abusers and create an inner dialogue in adulthood that mimics that of the people who may have gaslit them in the past, making it impossible for them to move into a place of self-neutrality. Let's start with an example to illuminate this process.

Yusuf's Story

Yusuf's older brother, Amir, was the "golden child" in his family. His parents doted on and praised Amir constantly. They talked freely about his "unlimited potential" to each other and in front of friends. Yusuf not only grew up in the shadow of Amir, but he also sustained significant emotional abuse from his father, who likely had undiagnosed narcissistic personality disorder and seemed to see his sons as appendages of himself rather than individual beings with their own unique strengths and talents. He was a physician and believed Amir had "what it took" to follow in his father's footsteps. Amir was a straight A student, was a track and field superstar, and even looked like his father. Of course, Yusuf's dad took all the credit for Amir being so smart, talented, and handsome. "Just like your father!" he would say with pride.

Yusuf, on the other hand, embodied more of his mother's traits. He was gentle, thoughtful, and kind. This made his father see him as weak. He repeatedly expressed shame and embarrassment toward Yusuf, calling him names like "little sissy boy." His father teased and taunted him and encouraged Amir to join in the abusive behavior.

Yusuf's mother struggled with chronic physical illness and a prescription drug abuse problem, so she was frequently unavailable to intervene in Yusuf's abuse or attend to her son's emotional needs. In fact, she often sought out Yusuf's help in managing her own care needs since her husband and Amir would not do so, despite the clear support she needed. Being a naturally kind and empathic child, Yusuf saw it as his responsibility to care for his mother. Rather than participate in extracurricular activities like Amir, he often spent his time outside of school caring for his mom.

The messages Yusuf received about his worth as a human were both overt and covert. While his father and brother gave him very direct messages—such as "You're a sissy," "You'll never amount to anything," and "You're no son of mine"—he also received covert messages from his mother. While she never said, "You are responsible for taking care of me," she certainly made him feel that caring for her was his job. She also never said, "I love you because you do so much for me," but Yusuf internalized that message and believed taking care of people was how he "earned" love and affection.

Understandably, Yusuf developed considerable negative self-talk in adulthood. Despite his emotionally abusive upbringing, he grew into a brilliant, kind, and talented adult who owned a successful business, had a master's degree, and participated in volunteer projects in his community. Ultimately, Yusuf distanced himself from his family and had virtually no interaction with them outside holidays or important family events. Despite this distance, his childhood emotional abuse continued to plague him because his own self-talk was now acting as his abuser.

Although Yusuf knew in his heart that he was a good, smart, capable person, he could not shake the belief that he was also a failure, an embarrassment, and unworthy of love from others unless he was doing something for them. He became the hero to everyone around him and never asked anyone for anything, fearing he would be rejected if he ever asked someone to provide for him the kind of support he regularly provided for them.

In this way, Yusuf began to "gaslight" himself. While he logically knew the truth about himself, he could not connect emotionally to that truth, so he continued to reinforce the abusive messages of his childhood to himself over and over: "No matter what I accomplish, I will always be a sissy loser." "I must earn love and support from others by doing everything I can for them, no matter how difficult or inconvenient it is for me." "Nothing I do will ever make me worthy. I have to fool people into thinking I'm a worthy person."

Nobody in Yusuf's adult life was abusing him anymore. Objectively, he was an exceptional man. Even his father warmed up to him as he became more and more successful (taking all the credit for it, of course, just like he did with Amir). Try as he might, Yusuf couldn't stop gaslighting himself despite all the evidence of his worthiness.

Yusuf's story is not an uncommon one. Many childhood trauma survivors take on the abuser role for themselves in adulthood. They perpetuate their self-hatred and suffering by convincing themselves that they are worthless, bad, unlovable, or total failures despite what is objectively true. They insist the lies they tell about themselves are the truth, which in a way is the very definition of gaslighting: insisting the truth is not real, and the lies are the truth. They create the "crazy making" for themselves and keep spinning in a cycle of self-doubt, insecurity, self-loathing, and despair. If you can relate to this, I'm sure you know how hopeless and exhausting it can feel.

Stopping the Self-Sabotage

So, how can you stop gaslighting yourself? Well, you're going to have to use the power of your mind to change your brain. Yes, you read that right. Let me explain.

We've already discussed how the amygdala and hippocampus interact when a trauma trigger is activated. Now I'd like to introduce two other areas of the brain, the cingulate cortex and the insula. Then I will discuss how to use your prefrontal cortex to mediate the unhelpful functions going on in your brain when you get triggered.

The cingulate cortex is the self-regulation center of the brain. It helps us regulate our thoughts and emotions, and it's responsible for good decision-making and judgment. When it's strong, it can help "downregulate" the amygdala, meaning it reduces the amygdala's reactivity to trauma triggers. Meditation and mindfulness can improve functioning in the cingulate cortex and improve its ability to communicate with the amygdala and prefrontal cortex.

Now, let's discuss the insula, which is the interoception center of the brain. Interoception is our ability to sense internal signals from the body. Thanks to interoception, we know when we are hungry, tired, hot, or cold. This is an important function for survival, but in the traumatized brain, the insula can become hyperactive or underactive. When it's hyperactive, we are prone to emotional reactivity and outbursts. When it's underactive, we are vulnerable to numbness and disassociation. While a healthy insula allows us to feel safe and present in our bodies, a traumatized insula creates the feeling that the body isn't a safe place to inhabit. It's why so many trauma survivors find meditation and other exercises in which they are asked to "sink into their body" so intolerable.

When a traumatized insula makes it hard to reap the benefits of meditation, we need to activate the power of the brain's thinking center, the prefrontal cortex. As you learned in chapter 5, the prefrontal cortex plays a primary role in higher-order cognitive functions. This includes decision-making, concentration, empathy, and social intelligence. It is also involved in self-awareness, self-regulation, and personality. Since the prefrontal cortex is where our self-awareness resides, we must learn to harness its power and become aware when we're engaging in self-judgment and stop believing the lies created by our traumatized brains. Then, we can lean into the self-neutral state of a healing brain.

Let's apply this idea to the concept of self-gaslighting. First, I want you to identify the ways you gaslight yourself in the present. Examples of self-gaslighting include:

- Blaming yourself for the abuse you endured as a child.
- Telling yourself that what you experienced wasn't trauma, wasn't a big deal, or wasn't really that bad. (Remember, your brain is trying to help you reconcile what happened, but it's accidentally making you feel worse about yourself instead of feeling better about the trauma.)
- Telling yourself you're being dramatic or too sensitive (or any of the other empathy-lacking messages you were told about yourself from your abusers or other adults in your young life).
- Questioning whether you remember the trauma accurately. (It's true that you may not recall all the facts or have a perfect recollection of the series of events, but that doesn't matter at all. So many trauma survivors will use the fact that their memories are fuzzy to discredit everything they remember or viscerally feel, and I need you to know that your body remembers enough of what happened to you for you to trust it.)
- Invalidating your trauma because "someone else has it worse." Let me tell you something: Someone is always going to have it worse. So what? This isn't a contest where

only the person who has it "worst" in the world is allowed to be impacted by their trauma.

- Believing your feelings aren't reasonable and beating yourself up for feeling upset by unpleasant situations (situations where it's probably very appropriate to feel upset, by the way!).
- Believing when someone treats you poorly, it is somehow your fault, or you deserve their mistreatment.
- Chronically apologizing for your actions even when you haven't done anything offensive.
- Second-guessing all your decisions or constantly seeking out the opinions of others before acting because you don't trust yourself to make good choices on your own.
- Assuming you're in the wrong when you have a conflict with someone and not speaking up for yourself because of that false assumption.

Since you're reading this book, you probably resonated with several of the items on that list. So, how are you going to get your brain to stop betraying you with all this self-gaslighting? You are going to train your prefrontal cortex to hop into action when you get triggered so it can direct the many activated parts of your brain to get in line and follow your instructions. The next section is going to tell you how to do just that.

Retraining Your Brain

In the traumatized brain, the prefrontal cortex doesn't always perform optimally when it's triggered, and it isn't always able to "reason through" a triggering situation. Therefore, if you want to retrain your brain, the first step is to teach your prefrontal cortex exactly what to do while you're in a calm state. That way, when crisis situations happen, your brain has rehearsed and is ready to jump into gear. The skill I like best for this is a trick from the DBT playbook: one-mindfulness. One-mindfulness teaches your brain to *listen* to your mind, instead of letting it spiral around on its own, all willy-nilly. This exercise is so mundane you'll probably find it useless and dull at first, but I promise you, this is how you teach your brain to do what you want it to do.

To practice one-mindfulness, all you need to do is choose a simple activity to focus your attention on. Anything like folding laundry, taking a shower, or washing dishes in the sink will do. Then engage in that activity while staying completely present in the moment and not thinking about anything other than the task at hand. As you do so, your inner dialogue might sound something like this: "I am folding this shirt. I'm folding the sleeves into each other and now I'm folding the shirt in half. The shirt is blue and feels soft in my hands. Now I am placing the shirt in the pile of folded shirts I've made." You can say whatever you want to stay on task.

Seems relatively easy, right? Not so fast. Unfortunately, you will more than likely not be able to stay on task. Your brain will drift away constantly and become distracted by other thoughts, as brains often do. When you notice this happening, just say something neutral to yourself, like "Oops, I drifted away, time to come back to folding laundry." And then you start over.

Don't get mad at yourself if this is harder than you expect it to be, especially at first. Drifting off is normal, and it isn't helpful to beat yourself up during the learning process. (You've probably done enough of that in your life as a trauma survivor, anyway!) I suggest imagining you are a kind teacher, gently guiding a new student on how to do an activity completely foreign to them.

The more you practice one-mindfulness, and the more you practice it with a variety of activities, the better your brain will get at listening to your mind. Your brain will begin to understand that your prefrontal cortex is in charge, and it must wait for directions before springing into action. Remember to get proficient at one-mindfulness during neutral moments if you want your brain to respond favorably to your mind in high-stress moments or crisis situations. That's when you will really see the benefits of neutrality in action!

Eventually, you will be able to identify when your brain is gaslighting you, and you will be able to use the power of your mind (your prefrontal cortex, that is) to say, "No. That's not helpful and we aren't doing that. We will do the opposite of that." You can practice turning self-gaslighting statements into more accurate, neutral statements that help you feel more neutral about yourself. Here are some examples of this:

Gaslighting Thought	Counterbalancing Thought
"I can't believe I did that! I'm such an idiot!"	"I'm not an idiot. My brain just got triggered and couldn't make the most effective choice. Now that I've identified what's happening, I can make a better choice."

Gaslighting Thought	Counterbalancing Thought
"I'm such a loser. This is why no one likes me!"	"I'm not a loser. Several people like me. I'm just being hard on myself right now because I'm triggered. I understand what's happening in my brain right now and I know why it is turning to self-criticism. I'm going to choose self-neutrality instead because it's more helpful and more aligned with reality, even if it doesn't feel that way in this moment."

Utilizing this strategy, you will eventually get better at responding to your negative self-talk and your triggered self in a much more neutral way. Over time, you will find yourself better able to use the power of your mind to block unhelpful thinking when you're activated. This will allow you to maintain a sense of control over where your thoughts go in stressful moments. Ultimately, you will learn to see yourself in a more neutral light and engage in self-acceptance, have a realistic view of yourself, and make better decisions when responding to triggers in the moment.

Another way to train your brain to be kinder to itself is to keep track of your negative thoughts throughout the day. Simply take note every time you have a negative thought. You probably have more negative self-talk than you realize, but it's so commonplace you hardly even notice it.

This subconscious self-dialogue reinforces those deep grooves in your brain that keep you stuck in a loop of negative self-talk. Practice intentionally calling it out and telling your brain—literally—to stop it. Think of it like potty training a puppy. It requires a lot of repetition and redirection. You must keep saying to yourself, "No, I'm not going to talk to myself like that. I will talk to myself like this instead." Then give that puppy in your mind some positive reinforcement and a metaphorical treat with a statement like "Good job. We identified it. We intervened. It might not have been perfect, but it's a good start."

If you need help identifying your negative self-talk, put a few reminders on your phone throughout the day. When a reminder pops up, ask yourself, "How have I spoken to myself in the last few hours?" What statements have you made about yourself? Be specific and write them down. If you were in a business meeting earlier where a problem came up, you might have said something like "Oh, no. What am I even doing here? I have nothing to contribute, and I'm way out of my league. Any day now they are all going to figure out what an idiot I am and I'm going to get fired."

Make a log of these self-defeating statements and write down some counterbalancing thoughts to challenge the negative ones. Keep a pad of paper, a notebook, a day planner, or anything you can use as a journal close by. Doing this exercise is a crucial step on the path to self-neutrality. Don't simply just read about this exercise without ever trying it out. Self-neutrality isn't going to emerge from simply reading the words on these pages. You must seek it out with action and intention.

When I do this exercise with clients, I usually see one of two reactions. Some people naturally see how unreasonable and untrue their internal voice can be. Other people look at a long list of self-deprecating remarks and say, "Yup. This is me. I'm a total loser." If you're in that second group, don't despair. You are not the loser you tell yourself you are, and you are fully capable of being the peaceful, content person you long to be. It might take a little more effort, but you are fully capable of getting there.

Once you have a compilation of the negative self-talk you engage in, take the time to connect it to the negative core beliefs you hold about yourself. Dr. Aaron Beck, widely recognized as the father of cognitive therapy, describes negative core beliefs as distorted thoughts that people develop because of adverse early life experiences. These beliefs create a "cognitive triad" in which people form a negative view of themselves, others, and the world. This framework becomes a lens through which they see everything. It can taint and distort their entire life experience.

For example, let's say you have a negative core belief that you're unlovable. Every time a person in your life hurts, disappoints, or rejects you, you will see it as confirmation of how unlovable you are. Whether positive or negative, we can always find ways to validate and reinforce our preconceived notions. This means when someone hurts you, you won't consider the problem might be with *them*, not you. Even worse, you won't expect or insist that people treat you with dignity. You will accept all kinds of unacceptable behavior from others because you think your unworthiness is the reason people mistreat you. You don't feel worthy of love, kindness, and respect, so you will accept virtually any kind of behavior from others because you're just happy to have people in your life at all.

You can see how this sort of cycle plays out. You believe something negative about yourself, and it gets reinforced repeatedly because you allow it to. When others mistreat you, you see it as evidence that you are unlovable. This belief will be reinforced every time you are treated poorly by others. This traps you in a vicious cycle where you are mistreated by others over and over because you expect it, you *allow* it, and your belief system is attracting people who will exploit your insecurity and self-doubt.

We teach people how to treat us based on what we will tolerate and what we won't. The hard truth is that it's more likely others will mistreat you because you expect it and allow it. It's much less likely that it's a reflection of you being as unworthy and unlovable as you think you are. In the next section, I'll help you identify the negative core beliefs that keep you locked in this never-ending cycle of defeatism.

Identifying Your Negative Core Beliefs

Generally, negative core beliefs fall into a few broad categories: defectiveness, unlovability, safety, powerlessness, and responsibility. Let's look at these more closely and break them down. You may want to highlight the negative beliefs that resonate most for you.

Defectiveness

Those who have core beliefs related to defectiveness might think, "I am worthless," "I am not good enough," "I am stupid," "I am ugly," "I am bad," "I am a failure," or "There is something wrong with me." People who see themselves as defective have endured repeated life experiences that reinforce their lack of capability. They may have been the baby in a large family of successful older siblings, or they may have had difficulties learning or a naturally shy temperament. As adults, they may avoid conflict or be afraid to make decisions. They may lean on others to help them navigate through life or avoid doing anything they aren't confident they can do well. I used to joke about how "I only do things I'm already good at," not understanding this "joke" was an insecurity rooted in my childhood trauma.

Another common belief among trauma survivors is the idea that their trauma has damaged them so irreparably that they are no longer "normal" people. We can feel as if our trauma has forever rendered us broken, weird, twisted, or too "dark and ugly" to be worthy of connection with "regular" people. I want to take a moment here to share a little secret: Most humans have a dark side. Most of us have morbid thoughts from time to time. Most of us experience fleeting moments of rage or homicidal ideation, or thoughts of harming ourselves. Many humans have sexual desires that they find questionable or feel insecure about.

Trauma isn't what makes you weird. Being human makes you weird! You may blame your traumatic experiences for any thoughts, beliefs, or desires you find unconventional (and your experiences certainly may inform these things), but you should know that all humans experience shame and insecurities over any thoughts, beliefs, and desires they think are unusual.

As a person who has been honored to hear and hold space for the deepest, darkest secrets people carry, I can assure you, we are more similar than we know. Humans are curious about the same things. We fantasize about the same things. Some of those fantasies are wholesome, and some are violent, erotic, or morbid. We all have the capability of landing in a dark place, and we scare ourselves with our thoughts or passing urges at times. We feel shame, and we all wonder if we are "normal." I don't know what normal means when it comes to the human condition, but I think humans are fascinating, colorful, and strange. This goes for trauma survivors and people without significant trauma, so it's just one more thing that brings us together in the human condition.

Unlovability

People with core beliefs related to unlovability might think, "I am alone," "I am unwanted," "I will always be rejected," "I don't matter," "My needs aren't important," "People will only love me if I constantly do things for them," or "I don't deserve love." They may have had neglectful, abusive, or emotionally unavailable caregivers. These were kids who were rejected by peers and bullied at school. They grew up chronically receiving messages that they weren't accepted, valued, or important to others. As adults, they may be codependent, needy and clingy in relationships, or overly self-protective and avoidant of emotional intimacy. Hyper-independence can be falsely categorized as a sign of strength, when it's usually a sign of trauma.

Safety

Negative core beliefs around safety might sound like "I'm not safe," "People will hurt me," "I can't take care of myself," or "I'm in danger." This core belief is often associated with significant trauma. There may have been chronic abuse or neglect. Perhaps there was a lack of basic needs like food and shelter. A powerful single-incident trauma can cause this core belief, such as the death of a parent or a terrible accident that resulted in permanent injury. Ultimately, people who feel unsafe are fearful, anxious, and agitated adults. They are chronic worriers, and others may experience them as "taking the fun out" of any situation.

Powerlessness

People who hold core beliefs related to powerlessness may think, "I'm weak," "I'm helpless," "I am out of control," "I need to be in control," or "I'm trapped." This is another core belief that can emerge from abuse or neglect. As adults, these individuals may present themselves as apathetic, resigning themselves to whatever life hands them. "Well, there's nothing I can do about it," might be their response to even small challenges. Without intervention, these people may fail to live up to their potential despite how creative, smart, or talented they are because they lack fortitude when faced with adversity.

Responsibility

Finally, those with core beliefs about responsibility may tell themselves, "It's my fault," "I have to do this alone," "It's not okay to ask for help," "I can't trust anyone," or "I have to be perfect." Critical, perfectionistic, and demanding caregivers can instill this negative belief. If you grew up constantly hearing, "You should have known better" or "You're the older sibling, you need to set an example," then you might be an adult with a responsibility complex. People with this core belief are highly functional as adults. They often have successful careers and rarely ask for help. They may have difficulty admitting when they are wrong and get defensive when questioned. Their self-image is built on the belief that they must be perfect, or right, or know how to do everything. As you might imagine, this is utterly exhausting for them and those close to them.

Now, ask yourself which negative core beliefs you hold about yourself. You might identify with several, and that's okay. If you feel overwhelmed by the sheer number of negative core beliefs you hold, don't panic. I'm going to guide you through the process of changing them. Once you know what your negative self-talk sounds like and what core beliefs are driving it, you can make meaningful, lasting changes. Remember that much of your negative self-talk arises because you have a traumatized brain and *not* because there is anything inherently wrong, defective, or unlovable about you. This understanding allows you to see your struggles in a more neutral and accurate way. Turning "I'm a failure" into "I live with a traumatized brain" is a far more neutral way to think about yourself.

CHAPTER 9

Use Your Power of Choice to Release Trauma and Cultivate Self-Neutrality

Now you know that trauma happens when bad things occur and you are powerless to stop them. But that doesn't mean that you are powerless altogether. I like to tell my clients, if powerlessness is the birth of trauma, then choice is the end of it. This chapter is all about reclaiming some of that power for yourself.

Today's power lies in all the choices you have now, that you didn't have back when your traumas happened. However, it's common for trauma survivors to struggle finding their power due to a psychological phenomenon called *learned helplessness*. Learned helplessness occurs when someone experiences a lasting sense of powerlessness because they have been conditioned into believing they have no control over their circumstances. This is what trauma can do, leading trauma survivors to get stuck in their pain forever if they don't learn how to recognize and harness their power.

A classic example of learned helplessness is that of the young circus elephant, tied down with chains to keep him from escaping, try as he might. Eventually, this sad little elephant accepts his fate and stops working to free himself. Ultimately, he can even be tied up by a flimsy rope from which he could easily break free. But since his abuse has conditioned him into a state of learned helplessness, he accepts the rope as binding and does not try to free himself.

Take some time to consider the chains that have held you down. Have they turned into ropes? Are you accepting these ropes as chains? Many of us are operating under the presumption of helplessness in at least a few areas. Perhaps you believe it's your lot in life to never find true love, or you think that no matter how hard you work, you'll never be able to get a promotion. However, it's important not to blindly accept conditions that were once true as always true. You must evaluate your current circumstances and approach your life with mindful awareness and creative problem-solving. Things are not as they once were. You are smarter, stronger, and more capable today than you have ever been.

This leads to the concept of learned *optimism* as a replacement for learned *helplessness*. The practice of learned optimism requires you to accept that emotional well-being can be intentionally cultivated. It means you don't assume that people who are happy feel that way simply because their lives just happen to be working out swell for them. When you practice learned optimism, you acknowledge that your satisfaction in life is, in large part, your own creation, based on how you choose to perceive and respond to your circumstances. You acknowledge that you are not powerless, and even if your current situation royally sucks, you likely still have some choice and power available to you. You can use your learned optimism to make good decisions, respond in a healthy manner, and improve the situation in whatever way you can.

Here's an extreme example. Let's say you have been convicted of a heinous crime you did not commit. You've been sentenced to life in prison, and, despite your attorney's best efforts, all appeals have been rejected. With a heavy heart, your attorney tells you there is nothing more she can do. You will have to accept your fate: life in prison with no chance of parole.

This is a worst-case scenario come to life. You have a decision to make. You can give up entirely, succumb to depression, be miserable and angry, and live the rest of your life full of hopelessness and resentment. Or, after a period of appropriate and necessary grieving, you can choose to find a way to live a meaningful, satisfying life regardless of your very unfortunate circumstances. You could sign up for all the classes and work opportunities the prison system will give you. You could choose to mentor other inmates and be a leader in creating a better prison culture. Maybe you could even write a memoir about your experiences or become an advocate for prisoners' rights.

I once encountered a man in just this situation. The circumstances around his conviction were outrageous. He was in his sixties when I met him and had been in prison since he was a teenager for a murder he witnessed but did not commit. The justice system had failed him as a teen, and though he was up for parole several times throughout his life, he was denied each time. Despite all of this terrible misfortune, I was struck by how peaceful he was.

At the end of our conversation, he said to me with full sincerity, "Even though I've spent my life in prison, I've still had a good life." It was such a powerful moment for me. Prison had not hardened him. He remained a gentle soul who was well respected among both the inmates and prison staff. He was up for parole again, and I hoped so much for him that this time the system wouldn't fail him. Sadly, his request was again denied. But his learned optimism allowed him to maintain a good attitude and a peaceful heart, and find a way to create meaning in his life despite circumstances that could tear a person's psyche apart.

Hopefully, the challenges you face today are not that dire. You probably have plenty of power and choice over the direction your life is going. You have a duty to yourself and the young person you once were to lead the best life you can.

Before you can lean into your power, you must first accept the past and process the emotional pain you continue to endure because of your early life traumas. I know many complex trauma survivors put a lot of effort into stuffing down, ignoring, and distracting themselves from their painful emotions. Unfortunately, that is never effective in the long term because those feelings always come out somehow, and usually it's in your interpersonal relationships. People who don't have a healthy relationship with themselves tend to struggle considerably with maintaining healthy relationships with others.

There are many ways to heal your heart and make peace with your past, but for most complex trauma survivors, it involves finding a great trauma therapist. So many clients come to me and say, "I've tried therapy, but it didn't work for me." If you are a complex trauma survivor, you need a therapist who is highly skilled in the treatment of trauma. You will need to interview therapists to find out if they are the right fit for you and your needs. Here are the questions you may want to ask:

- **How many years have you been a trauma therapist and what is your specialized training in the treatment of trauma?** You are looking for someone who is a licensed therapist, and who has been licensed for hopefully at least a few years, who can tell you the trauma treatment modalities they were trained in after they finished grad school.

- **How do you like to approach trauma treatment?** This is a question for you to determine whether you like their vibe and to see if you think their therapeutic style is one that could work for you.

- **What should I expect to feel throughout the course of treatment and how will I know when our time has come to an end?** Make sure they are being honest with you about how difficult trauma therapy is, that sometimes you will feel worse before you get better, and that they don't promise you will be "fully healed" when therapy is done.

- **Are you confident my experiences and mental health symptoms are in your wheelhouse?** Again, have they worked with other clients like you? Are they familiar with the unique struggles you face, such as chronic pain, eating disorders, addiction, or any other concerns you may have?

These questions should put you at ease in terms of your potential therapist's level of expertise in treating complex trauma. There are several well-researched treatment modalities they may use. You might hear terms like eye movement desensitization and reprocessing (EMDR), internal family systems (IFS), hypnotherapy, somatic experiencing (SE), or others. If you've never heard of the modality they use, ask them to explain it and look it up yourself to see what you think. If you already know of a modality you're interested in trying, feel free to ask them about it.

More than anything else, make sure you *like* the person sitting in front of you. Do you feel you can trust them with all your most vulnerable life experiences? Do they make you feel safe? Do you genuinely like their personality? It might sound strange, but looking for a therapist and looking for a romantic partner are similar in that just because someone is good on paper, doesn't mean they are the right person for you. The quality of the therapeutic relationship is more important than how experienced they are or what treatment modalities they specialize in. If you want the best outcome, trust your gut and choose a person you really like and trust.

Acknowledging All the Pain

One of the reasons trauma therapy is so helpful is because it allows deep reflection into your history. You'll come to understand who your true self is and how your trauma distorted your view of yourself, others, and the world, creating your wounded self. Developing a deep understanding of how your traumatized self was created piece by piece gives you the power to dismantle it piece by piece. There are many treatment modalities and exercises that can help you do this. One exercise I use was developed by a retired therapist, Marilyn Murray, who now works as an educator and consultant.

Her trauma treatment model, known as the Murray Method®, helps clients explore their past and make connections between their early life experiences and their current day struggles. Within this model is an exercise she calls the "trauma egg." It's basically a timeline of all a person's adverse childhood experiences. The trauma egg is broader than the ACE Survey, as it includes *all* painful life experiences. Not only does it cover specific traumatic events, such as the death of a pet or grandparent, the witnessing of violence, or sexual abuse, but it also captures subtler, pervasive experiences, like living in poverty, constantly moving or changing schools, struggling with a learning disability, and the like.

Because complex trauma survivors frequently struggle to determine whether their experiences are "big enough" to warrant inclusion on their timeline, I tell my clients, "If it left a negative impact on you, and it popped up in your mind when recounting your childhood trauma, it belongs on the egg." Using self-compassion as our guiding principle, we recognize that any painful, lasting childhood experience is important and worthy of honoring—no matter how insignificant we tell ourselves it was in retrospect.

Some people can't help but say, "But isn't that just life? Bad things happen to everyone!" Well yes, that's true, and each of those bad things shaped us. Just because bad things happen to everyone doesn't mean we aren't allowed to have feelings about the bad things that happened to us. Hurt and pain are part of the human experience. It's what connects us to other people, so honoring it allows us to empathize and identify with others. Minimizing it makes us dismissive and isolates us from others.

Sometimes I will also hear, "But what about people with terrible childhoods? There are kids out there who are being seriously abused or who are homeless and starving. My childhood wasn't that bad. I can't complain." I'm honestly surprised by how often my clients with severe trauma say this. You don't have to earn your right to have emotions. If something made you sad, scared, or embarrassed, or sent you the message that you were unworthy or unimportant, then it mattered. It harmed you, and you get to have feelings about it.

Telling yourself (or anyone else) that they "shouldn't" feel the way they do is about the most unhelpful approach out there. You feel what you feel. Emotions aren't "right" or "wrong"; they just are. You can tell yourself, "Sure, I was bullied by Nate as a kid, but I didn't know what he was going through. It turns out his dad was an alcoholic and was beating him, so it makes sense that he was a bully. I shouldn't have taken it so personally." It may be helpful to your healing process to practice having empathy for someone who harmed you, but using that empathy to undermine your experience is not beneficial. It really doesn't matter to the eight-year-old version of you that Nate had a difficult home life. Seeing that in retrospect will not change the painful emotions you experienced at the time or shift the negative messages about yourself that you internalized and carried with you into adulthood.

It's much more healing to recognize how painful your experiences were. Honor the pain with loving-kindness and empathize with the young version of you. Validate the messages you internalized as a child. They may not have been true, but they felt real at the time. "Yes, it makes sense that I thought I was unlikable when Nate bullied me. That was so painful. I feel empathy for my young self. I *was* likable, but it was hard to see that when I was being treated so terribly by a peer. I have been carrying that ugly message with me ever since. I can acknowledge now how the message I internalized was not a true message but, rather, a message handed to me from a difficult life experience."

When you can reframe your experience in that way, you use your adult wisdom to prepare yourself to let go of that old, untrue message and replace it with a healthier, more realistic message. Indeed, coupling that compassion for yourself with compassion for those who have injured you can be helpful in engaging the wisest part of you. Just don't skip over self-acknowledgment.

Comedian Donni Saphire once wrote, "Be kind to yourself, first as a prank, but then for real." Those of us who have discovered self-kindness and self-compassion know how completely stupid it feels in the beginning. We have also discovered that, over time, it really works. We feel better eventually because regular self-compassion practices truly change the brain.

Applying the Murray Method

Hopefully, you feel open to hearing how you can create your own trauma timeline. While there are many ways to write a trauma history, Marilyn's trauma egg involves drawing a large oval on a big piece of paper. The oval is the "egg," which is a metaphor for you. You are the egg. Your traumas are the cracks in your egg, or more literally, the cracks in your self-concept and worldview. As an EMDR therapist, I love this exercise because it identifies all the traumatic memories and negative core messages you can target during trauma processing.

As a therapist walks you through your trauma egg, they help you define your traumas (the events) and then break down the meaning (messages) you attached to those experiences. The therapist does this by identifying what happened to you (and how old you were when it happened); what emotions you felt at the time; what messages you internalized about yourself, others, or the world; how you coped with the trauma at the time; and what you needed that you didn't get.

Using this model to help you connect all your difficult early life experiences produces an objective, visual compilation of the themes that emerged from your journey. These themes created the negative core beliefs you identified in chapter 6. Laying it out on paper can produce an understanding of how you came to see yourself, others, and the world the way you do. It also helps identify how you developed unhealthy coping skills and how those coping skills were reinforced over time.

Let's return to the example of being bullied by a peer named Nate. Here's how that might look on the trauma egg.

For each event in the egg:

- **Age**
- **Event**
- **Emotions**
- **Messages**
- **Coping**
- **What you needed**

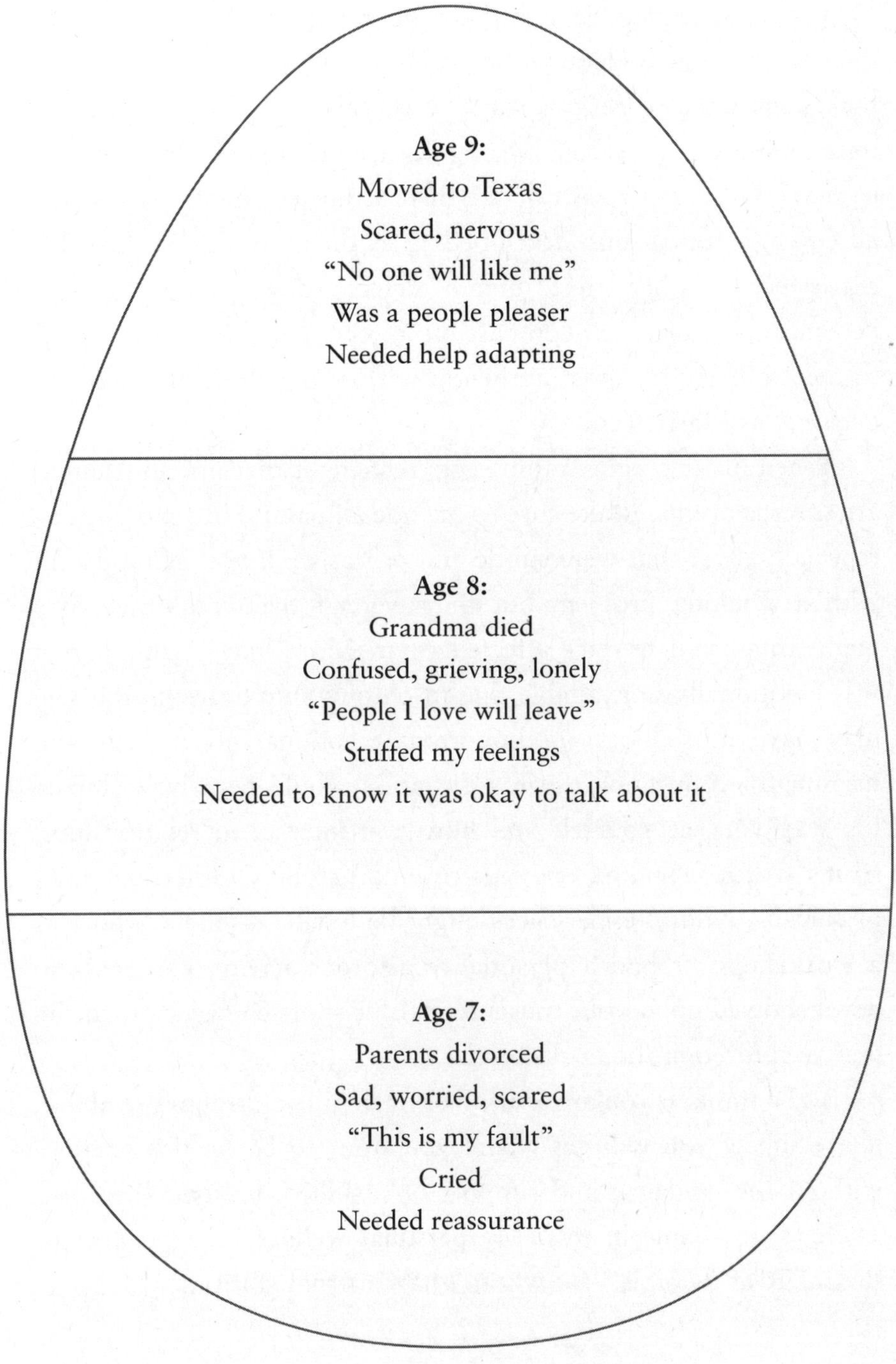

Age 9:
Moved to Texas
Scared, nervous
"No one will like me"
Was a people pleaser
Needed help adapting

Age 8:
Grandma died
Confused, grieving, lonely
"People I love will leave"
Stuffed my feelings
Needed to know it was okay to talk about it

Age 7:
Parents divorced
Sad, worried, scared
"This is my fault"
Cried
Needed reassurance

I love watching the lightbulbs go off as clients put together their trauma egg. Suddenly, they can say, "It wasn't all my fault. It makes sense that I feel this way!" I use this tool to shift a person's questioning from "What's wrong with me?" to "What happened to me?" Once a person can see their struggles and "weaknesses" as coping mechanisms developed as a direct result of their life experiences, rather than innate defectiveness, self-compassion becomes possible. Self-compassion is the path we must travel to meet our truest, most authentic self, or our "healthy balanced person," as Marilyn coined it.

When making your trauma egg, remember that not all traumas are specific events. Make sure to include all painful life experiences, especially those that were subtle and pervasive. If you had a parent with a drinking problem but they weren't overtly abusive, you might think you weren't affected by it. More likely, your parent was emotionally unavailable due to chronic intoxication, and you may have missed out on important emotional attunement and meaningful connection. Such a situation would negatively impact the way you see yourself and how you interact in relationships, so it's worth including on your trauma timeline. Other examples of chronic, painful experiences might be having a parent who was a workaholic or had a personality disorder, having parents who never showed up at your music recitals or sporting events, or being criticized for your looks or abilities.

To be frank, if you are a survivor of significant trauma or abuse, it is unlikely you will get where you want to be on this exercise without the guidance and support of a skilled, licensed therapist. There is no shame in this. My personal wellness is a product of several great therapists for whom I have eternal gratitude.

I would not have wanted to make my trauma egg alone. I needed the support of a therapist who could walk that painful road with me, keep me grounded, help me process my experiences, and make sense of things along the way. A skilled therapist will make sure you don't get too emotionally overwhelmed, which can happen when doing a chronological timeline of your trauma. They will give you tools for managing the painful emotions that come up as you do the work and make you feel cared for, validated, and connected to someone through it all. They will also make sure you don't rush through, ignore your feelings, and fail to do the processing necessary to heal.

Think of it this way: If you were diagnosed with a potentially fatal disease, would you decide to treat it yourself with the guidance of a self-help book on clean eating and healing meditations? Probably not. More likely, you would recognize the seriousness of the situation and seek the counsel of a medical professional specializing in the treatment of that disease. Trauma shares some similarities in that successful healing often requires you to employ the wisdom and guidance of a specialized health care professional, a.k.a. a highly skilled trauma therapist.

Becoming the Parent You Needed

When healing from your childhood adversities, you must first understand the origins of your unique struggle. Once you understand why you think and behave the way you do, the real work begins. With your newfound understanding, you must shift into compassion and kindly intervene on yourself. This is where the process can get tricky.

Part of the difficulty lies in the disconnect that can exist between your adult identity and your child identity. You might say, "Well sure, I understand why that little kid was struggling, but I'm an adult now. I should know better!"

Should is a very dangerous word. We tell ourselves we "should" know a lot of things we don't know. We "should" just get over it, or we "should" behave differently than we do. We "should" know better. But should we? Based on everything we have learned about ourselves, others, and the world from our early life experiences, we may or may not know things that would be helpful.

Age itself is not a reason we should expect to know something. We can't possibly know things that have not been properly taught to and ingrained in us. No amount of aging will magically teach us what we need to know to be our best selves. We must have adequate learning experiences. Without proper teaching or modeling, there is no way to expect anyone "should" understand something, no matter how old they are.

Perhaps a ten-year-old "should" be able to read. But if a ten-year-old has grown up working the fields on their family property instead of going to school, how could they be expected to be literate? Maybe a twenty-five-year-old "should" know how to file their taxes. The truth is, they may or may not know how to file them depending on what they were taught about managing their finances. The same rings true for how we respond to stress, deal with conflict, manage our emotions, and handle our interpersonal relationships. We only know what we have learned, and we can't possibly know what we haven't learned. We can criticize ourselves and each other for not knowing what we "should" already know, but we will never shame ourselves into learning anything.

Maya Angelou said it perfectly: "Do the best you can until you know better. Then when you know better, do better." The only way we can expect ourselves or anyone else to be proficient at anything is through learned experiences. When we have trouble with something, it is simply because we have not yet had enough opportunity to practice and become proficient.

One could argue that we "should" all know that eating a pint of ice cream when we're sad is not the most helpful thing to do. But if, in childhood, someone did not have a healthy adult to adequately teach them how to identify upsetting feelings and self-soothe in constructive ways, they might have had to figure it out themselves. A child has minimal capabilities for determining how to regulate distressing emotions without the guidance of an emotionally intelligent and responsive adult. And guess what? Eating feels good. Eating ice cream feels *really* good. If a child is left alone to determine how to soothe their emotions, they might just discover that eating sweets helps them temporarily feel better.

Further, it's likely they will carry this unhealthy coping strategy into adulthood if they are not presented with adequate tools for coping in healthier ways. Simply learning that sweets aren't good for you, or that emotional eating is "bad," isn't going to somehow instill healthier coping methods. When you're hurting, you're going to go back to the self-soothing tool you know works, even if it has negative repercussions. A person might feel sick, both physically and emotionally, after eating a pint of ice cream, but they will keep going back to it until they have satisfying alternatives they know will work.

This is where the concept of "reparenting" comes in. When you first begin your journey back to your true or "original" self, parts of you will be disjointed. There is a young, unresolved, broken part within you, as well as a wiser, healthier adult part. These parts need to be integrated. Once you identify your triggers and can see your unhealthy behavior for what it is, you need to "reparent" the young part of you. Essentially, you must provide for yourself the emotional support you needed back then that was unavailable. You must become the healthy, loving adult for the wounded child part of you.

If you struggle with emotional eating, you must learn to comfort yourself in ways that are effective and permanently healing. That tub of Rocky Road is just a bandage for your painful feelings. It makes sense that you turned to food if using food for comfort was modeled in your home, or if no solutions for self-soothing were taught at all. Your job now is to be the stronger, wiser adult figure for that young child you once were. You must learn to say to yourself, "I know this is hard. This hurts. Eating ice cream might mask my pain for a short time, but it won't solve the problem. I'll probably feel worse after I eat it. I'm an adult with options now and I can figure out what I really need to heal this pain."

Just because you don't feel love for yourself does not mean you shouldn't try to treat yourself with love. Eating a pint of ice cream is arguably not the most loving way to treat yourself. Though it may temporarily feel good, it will likely be followed by more intense negative feelings, such as shame, hopelessness, or self-loathing. Making a "self-loving choice" often means not acting on what feels best in the moment. Sometimes the most self-loving thing you can do is something you don't want to do at all. It might be calling a friend and asking for help. It might be getting out of bed and going to the store or the gym or anywhere just to get out of your house and interact with people. It might be challenging yourself to do what you're most afraid of, like leaning into your social anxiety by signing up for a dance class or volunteering at an animal shelter.

Reparenting means you treat yourself the way a healthy, loving parent would care for their child. You set boundaries for your own good and maintain those boundaries even when they are hard. You offer yourself kindness, acceptance, and understanding while also saying no to the things that aren't in your best interest, while you search for healthier solutions.

Reclaiming Your Power

You had no power when your trauma occurred, but you hold all the power now. *You* get to choose how to live the rest of your life. *You* get to choose how to heal, when to start, and even *if* you want to embark on a trauma healing journey. You already know therapy is a great option. There are many different therapeutic modalities and types of therapists you can choose from to aid in your healing. You can choose to engage in self-compassion and self-kindness. You can create a timeline to objectively review how your self-hatred was born out of your trauma, and you can choose to use that understanding to develop empathy for both your child self and your adult self.

You have the option of using empathy to reparent the wounded child inside you so you can grow into the healthy, mature adult you long to be. You have the power to take the steps needed to move from self-loathing to self-neutrality. Your most important choice now is whether or not you're ready to act.

If your answer is no (whether it's "I'm not ready" or "I'm not ready *yet*"), that's okay. Being honest with yourself is a good thing. Perhaps you can ask yourself what would need to change in your life, or inside yourself, to be ready to choose a new path. Perhaps you are in an abusive relationship and you realize you need to get yourself to a safe place before you can do any trauma work. That's a wise decision, so the next step might be reaching out for help and making an action plan to get yourself to safety.

Or maybe when you're honest with yourself, you realize you are afraid to do the work because you don't know who you are outside of your identity as a trauma survivor. You're afraid of the expectations you might be held to if others perceive you as "healed." In this case, the next step may be to engage in self-exploration to figure out who you want to be in a healthier life and to create a plan to make that version of yourself possible so that you feel safe to begin the work. Whatever you need is okay. Any amount of time you need is okay. You mustn't follow anyone else's plan or anyone else's timeline. You had no control during your trauma, but you get to have all the control in your healing.

In my work with clients, I have found that DBT skills training can be helpful for those who aren't yet ready to dive into the deep end of trauma work. Remember, there are four components of DBT—mindfulness, distress tolerance, emotion regulation, and interpersonal effectiveness—which are usually taught sequentially. The D in DBT stands for *dialectical*, and it refers to the idea that we can hold two seemingly opposing truths in balance. For example: "I feel unworthy" *and* "I know I have worthwhile traits." Or "I'm doing the best that I can" *and* "I know that I need to do better."

During the mindfulness module of DBT, you learn how to embody the concept of "wise mind," which involves being able to hold your emotions and logic simultaneously. In this state, you can acknowledge your feelings while responding to them in a logical, reasonable way. You can be both smart *and* unsure, willing *and* fearful, loving *and* angry. When you can keep all your truths in balance, you make the best decisions. This is why mindfulness is the first module in DBT.

When I teach clients DBT, I either teach distress tolerance or interpersonal effectiveness after mindfulness, depending on which area is causing more problems for them at the time. The distress tolerance module gives you tons of ideas for distracting and soothing yourself when you've hit your breaking point so that you have a plethora of options in times of acute distress. The interpersonal effectiveness module provides concrete skills for people who are concerned about the quality of their relationships and who want to improve their communication skills. Finally, the emotion regulation module offers a path to forging "a life worth living." You learn to recognize that pain and suffering will always be a part of life, but that doesn't mean you can't have a satisfactory life and feel good about yourself. I will discuss emotion regulation in more depth soon.

I encourage many of my clients to get a DBT workbook because the skills are generally self-explanatory, the concepts are easy to understand and mostly easy to implement, and because having a toolbox of internal resources before starting and during trauma therapy is always a good idea.

CHAPTER 10

Build a Tolerance for the Good Stuff in Life

When working with complex trauma survivors, therapists have a few traits they look for in the beginning of treatment, one of which is a client's window of tolerance. Some clients have a very small window of tolerance, meaning the amount of distress they can experience before having an outburst, experiencing an anxiety attack, or shutting down completely is quite small. In this case, we need to build their tolerance for handling distress. Other clients have a huge window of tolerance, meaning they can be surrounded by chaos, unacceptable behavior, and boundaryless people but still think, "I'm fine, this is fine"—until they hit a wall. It's only then that they realize how *not* fine everything is, and they begin to melt down. In this case, we need to reduce their window of tolerance to eliminate their tendency to tolerate the intolerable.

Another issue we consider is how well a client can tolerate favorable experiences. Think of how this applies to you: How easy is it for you to take a compliment? Does it make you feel good inside or uncomfortable? How long can you enjoy a pleasant moment or an extended period of happiness before you start worrying about when the other shoe will drop? Are you the kind of person who unintentionally sabotages the good in your life? If you are, it might be because you have a small window of tolerance for the good stuff life has to offer. Maybe it starts feeling scary when a new romantic relationship begins to feel safe, so you do something to blow it up. Perhaps things are going great at work and then you begin making careless mistakes. It's very possible you don't even realize you are engaging in these behaviors, but being present and comfortable in positive emotional states can be challenging when you're a trauma survivor.

So, how can you cultivate more neutral responses to build your tolerance for the good stuff? This chapter is going to help you do just that.

Facing Your Fears

In order to build your window of tolerance and move into a more neutral state, you first need to examine your relationship with fear. Like it or not, fear is going to be part of this process. You can't embark on a self-growth journey and avoid feeling fear. Fear is the emotional equivalent of growing pains. It is natural and necessary but, yes, it can be unpleasant.

Some people have such a strong aversion to fear that they run in the other direction every time they experience it, without properly evaluating if the concern is appropriate. The first step in facing your fears is to simply breathe. When fear wells up inside you, take a deep breath and let it out very slowly. Then do it again. It's important to slow down your autonomic nervous system (the part of your nervous system that controls involuntary processes like heartbeat and breathing), so you can stay connected to your wise mind in the face of fear. You won't see things clearly or make wise decisions if you go into a fight-flight-freeze response. So first, slow your body down.

After you have taken some slow, deep breaths, ask yourself, "What am I afraid of? What is the worst thing I think can happen?" People often stop themselves from playing out their "fear story" to the end—to their imagined worst-case scenario. However, if you just give yourself permission to explore the fear, you might learn that this worst-case scenario isn't that big a deal.

Let's say you started a new job several months ago, and there are many things you like about it. The people you work with are wonderful, the pay is good, and you really enjoy the work. Some things are troubling, though, and you want to tell your boss that everything isn't working out the way you expected. Perhaps you were hired in a sales position, and it was described to you as a forty-hour-per-week job. You've come to find that part of your work involves customer service and business development past the point of sale. You work about fifty hours a week due to the extra job functions. You want to define the expectations of your role and either have work delegated elsewhere so you can stay focused on the job you were hired to do or be adequately compensated for the extra hours you put in every week.

When you think about going to your boss to make this request, your heart starts pounding. Your palms sweat, and your mouth goes dry. You can't imagine getting the words out eloquently. You just know you are going to stutter and fumble, and it's going to feel awful. You don't want to do it. Fear is telling you to stay quiet, to just tolerate the job no matter how bad it gets.

Your sense of learned helplessness tells you there is nothing you can do, and this is just the way life is. Employers are always going to take advantage of you, and you must accept it. This is where fear might typically stop you. Over time, it may get so bad that you end up quitting or being let go because you make too many mistakes. By not speaking up, you potentially sabotage a good job you could have flourished in if you had only advocated for yourself in the beginning.

You can choose to do something different in this scenario. You can take a few deep breaths, then ask yourself, "What am I most afraid of?" Is it the fear your boss will say no to your request? Okay, let's say she says no. Then what? Are you afraid she will treat you terribly for making the request or, worse, fire you? Okay, let's say she fires you. Then what? Objectively speaking, even if the worst happens—she gets upset with you and you get fired—can you live with that? I mean, obviously, losing your job would totally suck. It might temporarily make your life really challenging. Assuming you don't have a sizable savings account, it could create a period of real financial stress. That's a big deal and I don't want to minimize it.

On the other hand, let's say you've realized after only a few months that this job is not right for you. You've seen the true nature of your boss and learned that the company culture does not fit with your values or goals in life. In this worst-case scenario, your employment is terminated, but you don't lose your voice. You aren't a doormat. You can feel good about speaking up for yourself, honoring your self-worth, and being brave. Plus, chances are you would have quit this job anyway after many months or even years of being completely miserable, which probably isn't in your best interest. And honestly, what kind of tyrant fires someone just for bringing up a concern about job expectations?

Once you have evaluated the worst-case scenario, ask yourself what the best-case scenario might be. Maybe your boss says she didn't realize you were doing so much extra work and agrees to take some things off your plate. She may also agree to compensate you for any additional hours you put in each week. Jackpot!

Now ask yourself, what is the most *likely* scenario? Usually, the most likely outcome falls somewhere in between the worst-case and best-case scenarios. Maybe she will tell you that there are bugs to work out due to the rapid growth of the company or because of a recent change in ownership. It's possible everyone is feeling the pressure right now, and there isn't an instant solution to the problem. She might ask you to be patient and tell you there should be new staff hired within a few months to ease the burden.

In this scenario, you don't get your needs immediately met, but you do get some validation from your boss. You also establish yourself as someone who is willing to speak up, have hard conversations, and actively solve problems. You gain some respect from her, even if she seems a little exasperated. Remember, she is under a lot of stress too, but she needs strong people on her team. By advocating for yourself, you are letting her know you are a person of strength and possibly someone she can rely on in the future.

When you slow down and lean into fear rather than freezing or running away from it, you give yourself the opportunity to have a healthy relationship with fear, which involves accepting fear as a typical human experience. You want to have an appropriate tolerance for fear and not become overwhelmed each time it pops up because you exaggerate the experience. When fear says to you,

"Danger! Stop! Retreat!" you need to say, "Wait. Let's examine the situation. We might be able to handle this."

In most circumstances, you will find the worst possible outcome is that you're going to be uncomfortable for a temporary period. You might have to engage in an awkward conversation. You might have to disappoint someone or give them feedback that will be hard to hear (and hard for you to say). You might have a temporary rupture in the relationship that will need to be worked through.

These are all ordinary life experiences you can handle. The fear of discomfort is often worse than the actual pain of the feared experience. Think about how many times you have been terrified of something, and then once it's over, you think, "Hey, that wasn't so bad!" When you frame fear as a normal emotion everyone experiences, and one you are capable of tolerating despite its unpleasantness, it no longer holds power over you. You can accept fear as an emotion you will feel from time to time. You can tolerate and move through it.

There is profound wisdom in the acceptance of fear. Once you accept fear as a natural state of being, you stop being afraid of it. That's right. *You can stop being afraid of fear.* Sometimes no matter how long you wait or how much you prepare, the fear won't go away. That means you'll need to get used to doing things while feeling afraid.

Author Anaïs Nin has been attributed as saying, "And the day came when the risk to remain tight in a bud was more painful than the risk it took to blossom." Use your budding sense of improved self-worth to remind yourself that you deserve whatever reward lies on the other side of fear.

Self-worth can help you feel courageous. Accept that there will be pain in this process, and you can choose to move forward even when you're afraid. You deserve to blossom. So, make yourself a mantra. *I can do hard things. I am brave in the face of fear. Fear does not own me.* Whatever you must tell yourself to feel strong, capable, and valorous, say it and own it.

Your voice of trauma has been lying to you for a long time. You are not worthless, unlovable, unimportant, stupid, or any of that other terrible crap you say to yourself. You are powerful. You are strong. You are brave. Brave people feel fear all the time. They wouldn't have to be brave if they weren't scared. People who live big, bold, beautiful lives don't do so because they never feel fear. They do so *despite* their fear. They don't see fear as a reason to not do something good for themselves. They see fear as a reason to wrap themselves with warmth and understanding, give themselves a kick-ass pep talk, and get out there courageously doing the things they long to do. You have a young version of yourself who is still inside you, rooting for you, believing in you, and hoping with all their might that you will show up as the adult they have always wanted to become. It's time to make little you proud and adult you optimistic about the future.

Increasing Your Tolerance for Good

Let's discuss a few ways you can begin developing a healthy tolerance for distress and increase your tolerance for the good. The practice of *positive psychology*, a term first coined by Dr. Martin Seligman in 1998, focuses on well-being through self-acceptance, personal growth, and purpose. There are many practices you can engage in to increase positive thoughts and encourage a state of well-being. Moving from self-loathing to self-neutrality is an intentional practice. You need to be willing to try things that make you uncomfortable. You must be consistent with new practices even if you don't like them, until they start feeling pleasant and natural.

Author Yehuda Berg once wrote, "If you look for the bad, you will find it. If you look for the good, you will find it. ...Your experience of life is up to you." Essentially, both existences are accurate. The terrible parts of life are real. So are the beautiful parts. But most of life's moments are neutral. Mundane, even. As I mentioned earlier, our brains are biologically wired to focus on the negative for safety and survival purposes. To function from a place of emotional health and well-being, we must intentionally look for the good in life.

Even though the negativity bias wires us to attend to the negative, we have the power to train our brains to think more positively. We have this power thanks to neuroplasticity, which is the brain's ability to change and adapt to our experiences. We can use neuroplasticity to our advantage when we use the power of the mind to create changes in the brain.

Think of it this way. No one is born knowing how to play the piano. However, many people learn to play the piano very well by reinforcing their piano-playing skills over and over through memorization and practice. You can use this same cognitive process to be happier and kinder to yourself by attending to neutral and positive experiences with intention and by repeatedly engaging in self-affirming thoughts and activities.

Let's start with neuroplasticity. The more you engage with certain thoughts or feelings (mental states), the more consolidated those thoughts and feelings become, ultimately forming a consistent pattern of thoughts, emotions, and behaviors that you come back to time and again (neural traits). What does that mean? It means *your mind builds your brain*. So, when you repeatedly engage in hateful self-talk or respond to triggers in unhelpful ways, you get better and better at it. Your thoughts teach your brain how to behave.

Unfortunately, your brain has developed a real talent for being unkind to itself, leading it to focus on all your perceived weaknesses and replay a story of how you will never be happy because you don't deserve it and aren't capable of it. This is why the idea of self-love makes you recoil, because it is the opposite of everything you've trained yourself to believe. The good news is, you can use the power of your mind to teach your brain to be kind, loving, and compassionate toward itself, thus changing your neural traits from self-loathing to self-neutral, and perhaps sometimes even self-affirming.

Officially, the definition of neuroplasticity is the brain's ability to form and reorganize synaptic connections. This is especially true in response to learning or experience. Luckily, the brain maintains the ability to do this throughout your entire life, so even if you've been hating yourself since childhood, you still have the power to move into self-neutrality.

There are two types of neuroplasticity: experience-dependent and self-directed. Experience-dependent neuroplasticity is something we are all subject to, as it is neuroplasticity that develops on its own through life experiences. Certain parts of the brain naturally become strong and active (or atrophied and inactive) based on natural repetition.

For example, researchers found that London cab drivers have thick neural layers in the hippocampus, a region of the brain that creates visual-spatial memories. This makes sense because driving around London all day creates maps of the city in their minds, and the hippocampus needs to work hard to make that happen. These cab drivers aren't trying to create a strong hippocampus; it just happens naturally because of the activities they engage in every day.

This leads us to self-directed neuroplasticity. Frequent self-deprecating dialogue strengthens the amygdala, which controls how we respond to perceived dangers, and weakens the hippocampus, which stores our positive memories. To benefit from self-directed neuroplasticity, we must be intentional about engaging in daily practices that strengthen the atrophied parts of the brain that produce happiness, gratitude, and self-kindness. The following section provides examples of some daily practices that can help.

Make an Affirmation List

Lots of people cringe at the thought of making an affirmation list but end up really enjoying it, I promise. So, for this exercise, I want you to make your own affirmation list. You don't have to say them in front of the mirror every morning. (Though you might want to try; it really does work with practice!) When I assign this exercise to my clients, I encourage them to write a list of positive affirmations, one for each year of their lives. That means if you are twenty-nine years old, you write twenty-nine affirmations. I've instructed clients well into their seventies to do this assignment, so if you're older, I don't want to hear any excuses! The way I see it, the longer you've been alive, the more strengths you have developed.

There are a few things to keep in mind when putting together your list of personal affirmations. First, you should keep them in the present tense. They should also be written in the form of "I" statements. For example:

- I am smart.
- I am loyal.
- I am a good friend.
- I have beautiful eyes.
- I like my crooked teeth.
- I am a good teacher.
- I am an artist.
- I enjoy cooking for my friends and family.
- I have survived hard times.
- I am doing my best in life.

Keep in mind that you don't have to believe the affirmations fully, and they don't have to be 100 percent true, 100 percent of the time. For example, I wrote "I am kind" on my list, even though I know I am not always kind. I am kind *most* of the time, and I aspire to be a kind person, so it belongs on my list.

You can also add things you are working on. If you're actively working on being a more honest person, even if you haven't been rigorously honest in the past, you can write "I am honest" or "I'm working hard to be an honest person." You might even go so far as to write "I'm trying to forgive myself for my past dishonesty and be a more honest person now and in the future."

As you add affirmations to your list, you may reach a point when you think, "I can't possibly write anymore! There aren't any other positive things about me!" If you get to this point, ask yourself, "What would my family and friends say about me? What would my pets say about me? What would my higher power say about me?" Step outside your self-criticism and look at yourself through the eyes of those who would be more loving and less critical of you. What would your teachers, students, children, bosses, or coworkers say about you if they were instructed to list your positive attributes?

While I find writing affirmations most helpful when you focus on your innate goodness rather than your accomplishments, looking at the things you are proud of is also worthwhile. For example, I completed my undergraduate degree as a single mom of three children, going to school full time while also maintaining a full-time job. You better believe I'm proud of that! While I could put "I am educated" or "I am proud of my college degree" on my list, I first might want to think about what that accomplishment says about me. I believe it says, "I am tenacious. I am persistent. I don't give up. I do hard things. I am a positive role model for my daughters. I am a strong woman. I am powerful. I am driven. I have a great work ethic. I am determined." These are all examples of positive attributes represented from a single accomplishment. Focusing on who I am at my core brings about much more pride and self-worth than merely listing my accomplishments.

Set a Daily Intention

Once you complete the positive affirmation assignment, you need to decide what to do with your list. Some people choose to hang it in a place where they can see it every day, like a bathroom mirror or the refrigerator. You may wish to read it every morning and set an intention for the day, focusing on one or two affirmations. For instance, if one of your declarations is "I am nonjudgmental," you may say to yourself, "Today I am going to be nonjudgmental as often as possible" or "I am going to acknowledge myself with appreciation each time I am nonjudgmental toward myself today."

At the end of the day, you can take a moment to journal or reflect on your successes: "Today, I was nonjudgmental toward myself when I spilled coffee on my shirt. In the past, I might have been hard on myself and embarrassed, but today I was able to have compassion for myself and even laugh it off later in the afternoon. I'm proud I gave myself permission to be human and imperfect and didn't make a bigger deal out of it than was warranted."

When setting intentions, the goal is to focus on *successes*, even if you have some challenges. If you notice yourself being judgmental toward a coworker, you don't have to beat yourself up for it. Just turn it around: "I noticed I was being judgmental toward Lisa, so I shifted my thinking and offered her some help" or "When I noticed I was being judgmental toward Lisa, I paused my thoughts and internally offered her compassion and wished her well." Even if you were judgmental toward something or someone during the day, try to notice the moments that you weren't. If all else fails and you really struggled with your intention, you can always say to yourself, "I acknowledge I had a hard time being nonjudgmental today. I will notice when I'm judgmental and reflect on it so I can be a less judgmental person moving forward. I'm not perfect, but I am working to become a better version of myself, and I'm proud of myself for that."

Remember, you are doing your best. Life is hard. Personal growth is a process. Being your best self requires a lot of work. Be gentle toward yourself along the way.

Keep a Gratitude Journal

There are a few other positive psychology techniques I regularly use that I find particularly helpful. My personal favorite is keeping a gratitude journal. At the end of the day, write down one or even a few things that made you feel grateful. They can be things specific to the day, like "I'm grateful for the nice weather today" or "I'm grateful for the compliment my boss gave me on my latest project." It's also helpful to include the little things we often take for granted, like "I'm thankful for legs that allow me to work on my feet all day" or "I'm thankful for the existence of modern transportation so I don't have to walk everywhere I need to go."

One thing I encourage clients to add to their gratitude journals is gratitude toward themselves. Every day, think about what you appreciate about yourself or something specific you were proud of that day. "Today, I was proud of myself when I bought lunch for an unhoused person" or "I'm proud I stayed engaged with my husband in that difficult conversation and didn't shut down."

Again, feel free to acknowledge the little things that are often overlooked: "I appreciate how friendly and outgoing I am" or "I really love that I am helpful and encouraging of others. That's a great quality about me." Keep in mind that some days, this will be harder than others.

On truly terrible days, give yourself permission to lower the bar. Remember, nobody runs at their full potential every day, and you are no exception. Some days, your gratitude journal entries will include statements like "I'm proud I got out of bed and brushed my teeth today" or "I'm thankful I didn't tell anyone to shut their stupid face hole today."

It's okay. We've all been there.

Turn Your Affirmations into Art

Turn on some music that makes you feel happy or empowered and draw some of the things that you like about yourself. Draw the people who have been your personal angels: the mentors, family, and friends who have sent you messages of encouragement along your journey. Above them, write the message they have sent you. For example, a picture of your favorite high school teacher might hold the message "I believe in you." That's a gift you get to carry with you for the rest of your life, even if you never see them again.

In addition, draw your accomplishments, big or small. Write above them what that accomplishment says about who you are. For example, if you recently achieved your goal of walking a 10k, the message might be "I am determined." Draw your talents. For example, if you were asked to sing at a friend's wedding, that might hold the meaning "I am valued." Keep this drawing somewhere convenient so you can reach for it whenever you need a little self-affirming pick-me-up.

Begin a Meditation Practice

Meditation is a wonderful practice for using self-directed neuroplasticity to your advantage. In fact, research has shown that mindfulness meditators have increased gray matter in their brains, which reflects their skillfulness in attention and attunement. Meditation is a great practice for controlling your thoughts and teaching your brain to do what your mind tells it to do. Since meditation can be difficult for trauma survivors, I suggest you start by listening to guided meditations that are short, even only a few minutes long, and increase the length as it becomes more comfortable.

Approach this as a one-mindfulness skill, wherein your job is to just keep listening to the voice of the meditation guide and bring yourself gently back anytime your brain begins to wander. For added benefit, look up meditations on self-kindness, self-compassion, positive self-talk, trauma healing, or any other area you think would address your internal criticism. You don't have to close your eyes either. You can meditate while sitting on a park bench, looking at the trees, or walking in your neighborhood. Find what works for you.

Practice Body Neutrality

This whole book has been focused on self-neutrality in an emotional sense, but let's not forget that you can be neutral about your physical body as well. Sometimes in my yoga practice, I direct participants to focus on a body part they are thankful for and offer appreciation to it. It might sound like "Thank you, hands, for allowing me to work at a computer every day" or "Thank you, eyes, for allowing me to see the world I live in." The idea is to notice parts of your body for what they offer you rather than focusing on what they look like.

Sometimes I like to offer compassion or even an apology to a body part I've been unkind to. It might sound like "I'm sorry, stomach, for always looking at you with distain and wishing you looked different. You serve an important purpose in my life, digesting food and eliminating waste, and you work hard for me every day to keep my body properly nourished and healthy. I will try to do a better job acknowledging how much you do for me and honor your contributions to my well-being."

Reset Your Nervous System

When your nervous system is dysregulated, it's difficult to be mindful enough to practice self-directed neuroplasticity. Teach your body to soothe itself when it's triggered with exercises like focused breathing. For example, practice deep breathing from your diaphragm, allowing your belly to expand on your inhale and sink back in toward your spine on the exhale. Count during your breaths, exhaling twice as long as you inhale. You can also try alternate nostril breathing, in which you practice breathing through one nostril while holding the other one shut, and then switch nostrils. You may benefit from shocking your nervous system back into a regulated state by taking a cold shower, jumping into a cold pool, or simply dipping your face, hands, or feet into a bowl of ice water.

This is just a small list of things you can do to practice self-directed neuroplasticity and reset your nervous system. If you're interested, you can find plenty more examples on the internet or in books devoted to this subject.

I strongly believe every trauma survivor should learn skills for emotional and physical self-regulation as a part of their healing process. Increasing your tolerance for the good requires creating a calm, grounded nervous system that is ready to receive and embrace all life has to offer.

CHAPTER 11

Choose Your Goals and Foster Posttraumatic Growth

At this point, you should have a clearer understanding of why you are the way you are. Hopefully, you also feel validated, encouraged, and dare I say *motivated* to change your life. The next phase of your journey is posttraumatic growth. Reframing your thoughts and challenging the way you think about yourself, others, and the world isn't easy, but it's where your life forever changes for the better.

The concepts in this chapter are more clinical than in previous chapters. If you're like me and that kind of thing can be overwhelming, give yourself permission to read this chapter in small sections. I've added frequent subtitles throughout so that you can take your time and easily stop and start as you go. It might make sense to read some sections more than once to make sure you soak in all the material. Remember, the hardest parts of life are often the most rewarding, so you don't want to skim over this part of the journey.

Sometimes when I'm really struggling with the challenges life hands me, I like to remind myself that I have a 100 percent success rate for getting through difficult times. So far, nothing has taken me down completely. Not everything works out the way I hope or plan, and sometimes I've had to abandon ship entirely, but I have survived. I have overcome. I have recovered. I rise and fall like the sun, but I never fail to rise. You and I are alike in that way.

Part of what helped me rise time and again were the unhealthy coping mechanisms I developed over the years. We all fall victim to this. For instance, let's say a tired mom says no to her toddler when he asks for a treat. The toddler throws himself on the ground and begins screaming and crying. The exhausted mom doesn't have the energy for a tantrum and hands her son the treat. What did he just learn? Throwing a tantrum gets him what he wants. He just connected an unhealthy behavior to a positive outcome. What are the chances he continues to utilize this tactic? Pretty darn good.

This example highlights the way humans can come to depend on their unhelpful behaviors. That's what makes posttraumatic growth so challenging. We've reached the point of your journey where you must evaluate your own unhealthy coping mechanisms and be willing to shift out of them. Your brain will reject this notion. It will implore you to keep doing what it thinks is working. You will need to critically evaluate your behavior and examine both the pros and cons of continuing certain behaviors.

Let's say you get reactive and defensive every time someone offers you undesirable feedback. That behavior probably keeps people from criticizing you (which you want if you're already constantly criticizing yourself), but at what cost? Others may avoid getting close to you or working on projects with you. They may talk about you behind your back. They may want to be close to you but feel like you're always pushing them away. Wouldn't it be better to learn how to handle constructive criticism without defensiveness? The answer is yes, but it will require you to step out of emotionally immature reactivity and into grounded self-neutrality. The following concepts will help you do just that.

Soothe Your Inner Child

Because this work can be painful, it is essential to have realistic expectations as you move through your personal healing and growth process. Despite all the work I've put into loving myself, treating myself with kindness, offering myself forgiveness, and practicing self-compassion, I still have moments when I feel like a loser. I doubt myself. I tell myself I'm not smart enough, interesting enough, or talented enough. The voice of self-hatred in my head that I know isn't mine has imprinted itself on my spirit.

However, I have come to accept that it may never go away entirely. I try to love myself as much as possible, and I seek self-neutrality when self-love isn't available. I don't see the presence of my trauma voice as a failure or defeat. I see it as a scar that reminds me where I have been and how much I have overcome. I do my best to offer myself loving-kindness when that voice shows up.

At the risk of sounding cheesy, I like to think of it as the voice of little, hurting Heidi, reminding me she is still a part of me. She needs forty-six-year-old Heidi, with all her strength and wisdom, to show up and protect her. Sometimes I will internally say to her, "Hello there, sweet little Heidi. I see you. I feel your pain. I know you need me. I'm here." This helps me tap into my gentle, adult self. I can protect that young, frightened, vulnerable part of me from a place of balance and wisdom. I can be a wise adult, soothing my insecurities while remaining focused on what is true.

When I am my wisest self, I can say "Even if I don't feel it right now, I am smart, worthy, and capable. Also, this is hard. I'm scared, and I don't know what the outcome will be." When that's too difficult, I can say, "No matter how I feel about myself right now, I'm just a human. Humans struggle. I'm struggling now and that's part of the human experience." I create a sense of neutrality with myself. I might not be able to be loving or affirming in some moments, but I can acknowledge my humanness and connect myself to common humanity to foster self-neutrality.

I know it may sound silly to talk to your inner child in that way. You probably don't want to do it. By now, we both know how this goes. I understand the resistance, but I'm encouraging you to try it anyway. What's the alternative? Beating yourself up? Allowing fear and self-loathing control you? How's that been working out? Let's try a new approach, even if it feels awkward at first. The only way to change the way your brain thinks is to engage in new, healthier thoughts with intention. This is what that looks like.

Recognize the Dreaded Impostor Syndrome

When I was in graduate school, I must have had a million moments of uncertainty. "I'm not smart enough for this. I don't belong here. My professors are going to figure out I'm in over my head." It was the dreaded impostor syndrome, a psychological phenomenon in which people believe they are incapable and are going to be discovered as a fraud. Luckily, just knowing impostor syndrome was a real thing, common enough to have a name, helped me tap into my wise mind.

In the most trying moments, I said to myself, "I feel overwhelmed. I am unsure and afraid. I think the other students are having an easier time or are better at this than I am, but I don't have any concrete evidence of that. My professors would tell me if they were concerned about my work. I'm getting excellent grades and good feedback. It's normal to struggle and be scared as a grad student. I can do this. All the evidence says I'm doing fine. I just need to keep doing my best and push forward." This kind of wise-minded internal dialogue is essential for overcoming your self-limiting thoughts.

Set Your Posttraumatic Goals

Understand that impostor syndrome will be present, but it can't be the voice that guides you. Think about what you want your life to look like at some point in the future. It could be six months, a year, or five years from now. Write down five goals for where you will be in your life at this determined point in the future. Maybe you will have finished your college degree, bought a house, or overcome a debilitating phobia. Perhaps you want to create and sell a piece of art, write a book, or climb the Inca trail to Machu Pichu. Pick goals that are not dependent on other people, so getting married and having kids isn't a great option here. It's a lovely goal, but for this activity, I want you to focus on goals that are entirely within your power alone.

Be realistic. If your goals for the next year are to get into Harvard, complete an Ironman, and cure cancer, you might not be setting yourself up for success. I suggest including some small, easily attainable goals on your list so you can have some early success. Perhaps you want to master a challenging yoga pose or learn how to make the perfect omelet.

Now I want you to write down (or make a Word document, or use the Notes feature on your phone—you get the point) one thing you can start doing right now to move one step closer to each goal. "Start stretching for ten minutes every day," "Sign up for a community college class," or "Put fifty dollars a week into a savings account."

The trick here is to balance what is attainable with what pushes you slightly out of your comfort zone. "Doable but challenging" should be your intent. Too simple and you won't benefit from the deep satisfaction derived from achieving something difficult. Too complicated and you may not achieve the goal at all.

Finally, ask yourself, "What is getting in the way of me taking this first step right now?" Use your sense of learned optimism to find creative solutions to the obstacles in your way and motivate yourself to start with small steps in a forward direction. Once you have succeeded at this first step, ask yourself, "What small step can I take now to move closer to my goal?" If your first step toward mastering that yoga pose was daily stretching, your next step could be joining a yoga studio or attending a yoga class twice a week. Keep biting off one piece at a time, even if the pace is slow and even if you sometimes take steps backward before you can move forward again.

For example, if you get a hiking injury, you'll need to take the proper time and steps to heal completely before getting back to your training. That can be frustrating, but the passage of time will continue no matter what. You may as well spend that time working toward something that makes you feel accomplished or proud. Anything that allows you to feel less critical and kinder to yourself is a win.

Last, stay focused on what's working. Your brain will constantly look for what's wrong. You must train it to look for what's right. Earlier, I suggested shifting the question "What's wrong with me?" to "What happened to me?" Now is the time to shift "What's wrong with me?" to "What's right with me?" Identifying and harnessing your strengths is a crucial part of self-neutrality. If you want to embrace self-acceptance, you must know where your power lies and how to use the power inside you. What do you like? What are you good at? What's working now? What has worked in the past? Use neuroplasticity to your advantage and train your brain to find the positive.

Activate Your Wise Mind

One way to build an encouraging internal voice is to ask yourself, "Is this message coming from my trauma or my wise mind?" Alternatively, you can ask your wise mind a question and wait for it to answer. Again, this may sound cheesy, but the truth is, you have the answers inside you. Your wisest, most grounded self lives within you just as much as your fears and insecurities do. You can choose which parts of yourself to nurture and grow.

Ask yourself, "What would my wise mind say? Can my wise mind provide any additional information to consider or challenge my inner critic in some way? What does my wise mind want me to know right now?" Sometimes I'll ask myself, "If I was in my wise mind right now, what would I do? Can I do that now?" If I know I'm not capable of doing the wisest thing in a difficult moment, I'll ask myself what I can do that's closer to my wisest self and further away from my most reactive, traumatized self. There's no shame in doing the "next best thing." Any time you disrupt your negative patterns, even in a small way, it's a big success.

Perception Is Everything

Earlier, I wrote of Aaron Beck's cognitive distortions. His cognitive theory inspired the development of cognitive behavioral therapy, otherwise known as CBT. The premise of this theory is that people's *perception* of an event is more powerful than the *facts* of said event. Thus, changing the way a person perceives or thinks about a situation can lead to more neutrality, empowerment, and overall well-being.

Let's say you have been given a serious health diagnosis, like multiple sclerosis (MS). The prognosis for a person with this condition could be a loss of mobility and chronic pain. I knew a woman named Paula who was wheelchair bound due to her MS. She certainly could have given in to her negative thoughts and become severely depressed. In fact, she experienced a serious bout of depression shortly after getting her diagnosis, and she continued to struggle (some days more than others) with the limitations the illness put on her.

Most days, though, she carried a sunny disposition and chose to focus on all the things she could still do. Moreover, she intentionally honored herself every time she figured out a creative way to get things done. Paula couldn't do all the things she used to do, but she could still do many things. She found innovative solutions to the problems she faced.

Paula chose to look for and focus on the positive aspects of her life so she could still be a mostly happy, fulfilled person. On the days when her emotions got the best of her, when her challenges seemed too unfair and overwhelming to manage with a smile, she practiced self-compassion. Paula validated how hard it was to live with a debilitating disease. She gave herself permission to be angry. She cried. She reached out to friends and asked for help when she needed it. She went to a support group for people with MS who could understand and affirm her feelings. She practiced loving-kindness until she felt soothed, comforted, and strong enough to shift her thinking and focus on the good, or at least the neutral, once again.

Paula's posttraumatic well-being was not determined by her life's situation. She accepted MS was beyond her control, an unwelcome curveball that life threw at her. She made intentional choices about how to perceive her experience. She understood the emotions she felt about her illness were, in large part, determined by what she told herself about the MS experience. In other words, the meaning she attached to her thoughts dictated how she felt. If she chose to attach a negative meaning to her illness, like "My life is over" or "I'll never be able to enjoy life now," the sadness would become unbearable. She chose instead to reject those thoughts when they surfaced and use her wisdom to replace them with more helpful, realistic ideas.

The tactic Paula employed is called *reframing*, and it's a powerful skill for challenging cognitive distortions. Dr. Beck identified fifteen primary cognitive distortions that require awareness and intervention, which I describe in the section that follows. An instrumental part of posttraumatic growth is understanding the cognitive distortions you engage in so you can change the way you respond to your unhelpful thoughts.

I think it makes sense to read this section of the book twice. First, just read through all the distortions to grasp the definitions. Then, go through a second time and evaluate the ways you personally engage in each distortion. It might be helpful to rate them in order of how prevalent they are in your thought process. Remember, you can only grow if you have a deep awareness of your own dysfunction and are willing to acknowledge it and actively intervene on the unhealthy parts of you.

Filtering

When a person engages in filtering, they ignore all the positive aspects of a situation and focus only on the negative, essentially filtering out the positive. Suppose someone is coming to terms with the death of a pet. They might tell themselves, "I'll never love another animal as much as I loved Buster. I'll never be as happy as I was with him in my life. I'm never going to enjoy hiking or camping ever again because those were things we loved to do together."

Focusing on these thoughts keeps the grieving pet owner from acknowledging the positive truths that simultaneously exist with the negative: "Buster lived a long, happy life. We brought each other a lot of joy and were lucky to have each other. I'm so glad I was able to give him so much happiness, because he sure did the same for me. I have many beautiful memories of us together I will hold onto for the rest of my life. I will remember those times with fondness whenever I hike our favorite trails or camp at our favorite spots."

This is an example of healthy—not "toxic"—positivity. Acknowledging the positives doesn't take away from the negative truths. A person grieving the loss of their pet is entitled to all their sad feelings. In fact, it's healthy to feel their sadness fully so they can grieve appropriately and move on. However, if the pet owner filters out all the good because of their pain, they both perpetuate and magnify their suffering and lose the opportunity to acknowledge and celebrate the life of their beloved pet.

Polarized Thinking

Also known as black-and-white thinking, this all-or-nothing way of looking at a situation removes all the nuance that exists in the world. Let's say a woman introduces her date to one of her girlfriends. During the interaction, her friend makes a teasing comment, and the woman is embarrassed. She might say to herself, "I can't believe Nina made fun of me like that in front of my date. She was trying to sabotage my potential relationship! She is so two-faced and untrustworthy! I can't be her friend anymore."

It's possible this is a toxic friendship that needs reevaluation, but it's also possible the friend simply used poor judgment and didn't mean to be as hurtful as she was. Alternatively, the hurt friend may have been overly sensitive, taken the comment out of context, or misinterpreted its meaning. The truth about all human relationships is they are imperfect because they involve imperfect humans.

We all hurt people we love. We say things we regret and do boneheaded things sometimes. It doesn't mean we are bad friends or bad partners. It means we are fallible beings who need to correct our wrongs from time to time. If we cast off every person who ever hurts us as toxic or unsafe, we will end up very much alone. We will face a similar outcome if we fail to acknowledge the ways we show up as harmful in our relationships. It's important to examine the gray in all situations so we don't fall into black-and-white thinking.

A healthier reframe for this situation might be "Nina really hurt my feelings with that comment. I need to discuss it with her and find out what she was thinking. I want to share my hurt in a non-accusatory way so she can understand my point of view and honor my feelings. I care about this friendship, so I want to handle this appropriately and come to a resolution we both feel good about."

Overgeneralization

This faulty line of thinking happens when we take one situation and generalize it broadly across all conditions. I once heard someone say, "I dated a guy from New Jersey who cheated on me. Never trust a guy from Jersey. They're all womanizers." It's natural for our brains to want to categorize things. It goes back to our survival instincts. Our brains desire efficiency, and the primary goal is to keep us alive. The most efficient way to categorize things is to throw everything into "safe" and "unsafe" boxes so we can quickly move on and keep up that important business of staying alive.

There's a problem with this primitive categorization system, though. We are no longer cavemen trying to avoid death by lion attack or consumption of a poisonous berry. Our brains want to categorize and move on quickly. "Lion? Run!" "Puppy? Cuddle!" "Poisonous berry? No!" "Cheesecake? Yes, please!"

Guys from Jersey? Take a breath. The nuances of life in the twenty-first century are lost on the primitive brain's method of categorization. As such, we must work at training our minds not to rashly throw situations or people into the "unsafe" box based on one experience. This is good news for guys from Jersey—and for all of us.

Jumping to Conclusions

This distortion is exactly what it sounds like. When we jump to conclusions, we assume we know the outcome or the truth of something without having all the evidence. We are all guilty of this, and I am no exception. I've had trouble sleeping my entire life. My ex-husband begged me for years to get a sleep study or see a sleep specialist, but I stubbornly refused because "I knew" all they would do is prescribe me a strong sleep medication I didn't want to take. Finally, after years of suffering, I made an appointment with a sleep specialist and was pleasantly surprised at all the options provided to me. Being so sure I already knew what would happen when I lacked adequate data to support my theory caused me years of unnecessary sleeplessness.

Give yourself the gift of taking a beat before making a decision or dismissing someone's suggestions. You might be surprised at how much quicker you will solve problems if you remain open and less reactive to the solutions.

Catastrophizing

We catastrophize when we assume something is far worse than it is, like making a mountain out of a molehill. The examples here are endless. You said something embarrassing when you met your girlfriend's parents for the first time, so you're convinced they hate you and your girlfriend is going to break up with you. You forgot to do something your boss asked of you, so now you're sure you will be fired. Your teen hasn't texted you back in two hours, so something terrible must have happened.

This way of thinking is unhelpful in every way. How is obsessive thinking going to help the situation at all? We've already discussed how worst-case scenarios usually don't come to fruition. Spending all your mental energy hyper-focused on the worst possible outcome isn't preparing you for what will most likely happen. Instead, ask yourself, "What is the most likely outcome?" Spend your energy creating a plan for the most likely scenario. Better yet, rather than obsessing about the possible worst-case scenario, ask yourself, "What went well? What could go right?"

If you struggle to do this on your own, ask a trusted friend. It's often easy to see things with greater perspective when you aren't emotionally invested. If necessary, let someone else serve as your barometer until you get good at holding reality in balance on your own.

Personalization

This is a distortion in which people believe they are personally responsible for outcomes when they aren't. An amusing example of this is the superstitious sports fan. You know them (or maybe you are one!). They believe they must wear a specific clothing item or watch the game in a precise location for their team to win. Pretty harmless.

However, in more distressing situations, a person may believe they caused a negative chain of events through their behaviors or thoughts. "If only I would have answered the phone when she called. Then we would have talked for ten minutes, she would have left the house ten minutes later, and she wouldn't have been in that car accident." This example highlights how much responsibility we can assign ourselves for situations that honestly have nothing to do with us.

We mustn't believe we have the power to make significant events occur or not occur through simple behaviors (such as taking a call or not). The world is a jumbled-up place with things happening or not happening at random all the time. You are just a tiny piece of the puzzle. Like it or not, you don't control much. You are not responsible for happenstance. Good things happen. Bad things happen. You will make yourself miserable if you link all your actions to the bad things that happen around you.

Control Fallacy

If personalization assigns us responsibility, the control fallacy assigns us power. A person engaging in this distortion may believe they have more control over people or situations than they do. They may also assign power inappropriately to someone else. Let me give you an example to illustrate what I mean.

Let's say a married couple is arguing. Jasmine is getting really worked up because Maya is criticizing her in an elevated tone. Jasmine gets so upset she throws the remote control she is holding, and it breaks. Then she shouts at Maya, "You make me so crazy! I wouldn't have done that if you weren't yelling at me!"

No, Jasmine. Maya did not make you crazy. You gave yourself permission to act like that.

We all choose how to respond to adverse situations. If Maya takes responsibility for her partner's actions, she falls victim to the control fallacy. Maya can and should own that yelling at her wife was not healthy or productive. But she didn't make Jasmine throw and break the remote. Jasmine alone is responsible for how she responded to Maya's unhealthy yelling behavior.

When someone else is behaving badly, we are more likely to allow ourselves to do the same thing. In posttraumatic growth, we take ownership of our behaviors. Even when others are being unhealthy toward us, we have options for responding in a healthy way. When we do, it feels good, and we can establish pride in ourselves and see our growth in a tangible way, which helps us see ourselves in a much more positive light.

Fallacy of Fairness

I hate to break it to you, but the adage is right: Life is not always fair. If you are completely hung up on things being fair all the time, you will set yourself up to be both unhappy and resentful. To move through life with peace of heart, you must anticipate that "unfair" things will happen, and you must find a way to reconcile it.

Sometimes the lack of fairness in the world will work out in your favor, like if you run a red light but don't get a ticket or get in an accident. Lucky break. The laws of fairness let you off the hook this time, and you probably thought nothing of it. However, when something unfortunate happens, people often don't remember all the other times unfairness worked to their benefit.

When I was in college, a reckless driver randomly swerved out of his lane, sideswiped me, and sped away, leaving me waiting on the side of the road with a damaged car and wondering what on earth just happened. If I had been hung up on how unfair it was, I would have made a bad situation worse. Yes, it was unfair. I wasn't doing anything wrong, and I didn't deserve it. They never caught the guy, and he got away with it. The whole thing sucked.

Sometimes life sucks. I accept that life sucks sometimes and that, occasionally, bad things I don't deserve will happen to me. This attitude allows me to deal with the situation and move on with my life as quickly as possible without fixating on the unfairness and dragging out my own misery.

Blaming

Okay, time for total transparency. My hit-and-run story didn't end there, and I wasn't so zen about it. When the jerk who hit me sped off, I called 911 and started chasing him in my damaged vehicle. Obviously, this was a terrible idea. All hopped up on adrenaline and youthful determination, I was resolved to get his license plate. The 911 officer told me at least twice to stop chasing him before I accidentally rammed my car into a half-wall and finally stopped.

My situation ended much worse than it needed to because I refused to accept a moment of unfairness. Ultimately, I worked with the 911 officer to help the police find my location, and I made an official report. I was so angry. At that point, it would have been easy to blame the hit-and-run driver. "He made me drive into that wall!" I might have said with youthful indignation. But that wouldn't have been the truth. I hit the wall because I reacted terribly to an unfair situation. I wasn't being reasonable, and I'm lucky I only hit a wall and not a person.

Shoulds

Perhaps you've heard the colloquial phrase "Stop shoulding on yourself." This speaks to all the unspoken and sometimes arbitrary rules we assign ourselves and others. When we hold the world accountable for all the rules we make up in our heads, we set ourselves up to be disappointed and unhappy.

"He *should* have known I wanted to be invited to poker night." "I *should* have checked the tires before leaving on that road trip." "I *shouldn't* have spent all that money." You can endlessly "should" yourself and the rest of the world, but we're all just imperfect people doing our best. We aren't perfect at following our own rules, and others aren't going to be perfect at it either. To be truly content, we must accept imperfection and be willing to roll with the punches when we falter or when others disappoint us.

"Shoulds" aren't just about perfectionism. Sometimes they're more about the rules we create that don't make any sense. There is value in asking where our rules come from and questioning ourselves when our standards lack logic. Think about the old, unspoken rule that men shouldn't stop to ask for directions. How does that make any sense? What does being a man have to do with geography? It's just outdated toxic masculinity that helps no one. When we question the basis for our internal rules, we may find that some of our "shoulds" are immature, stubborn, or just plain nonsensical. How many times have you said to yourself, "I should have known better"? But how could you have known if you never had this exact experience before?

Emotional Reasoning

Emotional reasoning is the faulty belief that our feelings are facts. "I feel unsure about this work project, so I must have done a terrible job." "I feel fat in this outfit, so I must look hideous." "I feel hurt by my brother's words, so he must not care about me." You've probably heard it before, but feelings are *not* facts. They're just feelings. It is a fact that you feel what you feel, but despite how real something *feels*, intensity alone does not make it true.

Checking the facts is paramount to living in balance. Your brother's words may have hurt you, but what is the evidence he doesn't care about you? Is there any data that says he does care about you? Has he made you feel cared about in the past? What about the time he gave up his weekend to help you move or hopped on a plane to be there for the birth of your first child? We can't live in a vacuum with our feelings. It's important to acknowledge our current feelings while also tempering them with all the information we have gathered about a person or situation along the way.

Fallacy of Change

In this cognitive distortion, we tell ourselves we *could* be happy, but only if other people were to behave differently. You know, if my boyfriend was more considerate, or my boss was more understanding, or if only my ex were more reasonable about co-parenting issues, then I could finally be happy. Sorry, but things just don't work that way.

The fallacy of change is faulty thinking because in it, you give away all your power to some other person. You hand your happiness over to someone else in the hopes that they will nurture and grow it for you. Here's the problem: *That's not their job*. They are busy trying to nurture and develop their own happiness. You must take that power (and responsibility) right back into your own hands.

Early in my career, I contracted with the county family court. I worked with parents to sort through co-parenting issues. One thing this work taught me is that you must figure out how to be content despite the people in your life who might actively seek to irritate you. It's helpful to acknowledge, "This part of my life is extremely upsetting and annoying, but I can focus my attention on other parts of my life that are working out well and derive a state of neutrality from them."

Even in those moments when it feels like everything is falling apart, there are still a few things you can hold to that bring you some level of peace. Remind yourself with phrases such as "At least I can go to the park and watch the ducks swim around the lake. I feel peaceful there" or "I'm so thankful for my friendship with Jamal. I don't know what I would do without his support." If you must, identify the neutral things you appreciate, like "At least I have electricity" or "Thank goodness for popcorn and movie nights." Remember, counting on other people to show up differently is always a recipe for disappointment. You are more likely to find contentment when you value what others bring to your life despite their flaws.

If you are in a hostile situation in which you are stuck with someone for a while (for example, co-parenting after a painful separation), seek out relationships in which you don't feel so perpetually unhappy. Focus on those healthy relationships, and don't let the annoying ones have so much power over your well-being. When dealing with someone who really wants to make you miserable, it's quite satisfying when you refuse to let them have their way.

Global Labeling

When a person engages in global labeling, also known as mislabeling, they take generalization to the extreme. Let's say you bake your best friend a cake for his birthday. You follow the recipe step-by-step, but for some unexplainable reason the cake doesn't rise, it tastes weird, and it's not attractive to look at either.

A person who doesn't engage in any faulty thinking might laugh and say, "Welp, that was a disaster! It's the thought that counts, right?" A person who engages in generalization might say, "Well, I just can't bake. I'm never attempting a cake again!" But a self-loathing person who engages in global labeling might go right to an extreme response, like "I'm a total failure. I can't do anything right. I'm a worthless friend and person!"

In a moment of extreme reactivity such as this, it is helpful to employ self-compassion skills before checking the facts. When you have an emotionally charged response, practicing compassion can soften your experience of yourself and make you more open to using your healthy coping skills: "Wow, I'm really upset about this. I wanted so badly to do something special and have it turn out well. I'm heartbroken right now because this didn't turn out as I'd planned. I put a lot of effort into this, and my disappointment is overwhelming. It's reasonable to feel this way. It's okay to be upset when I want something badly, I work hard to make it just right, and it doesn't end up at all as I'd hoped. It's perfectly acceptable to be upset by this."

Once you have calmed yourself with self-compassion, then you can check the facts, reach out to a support person, or use another helpful coping skill.

Always Being Right

If you put your need to be right above the health and quality of your relationships, you are setting yourself up for a life of loneliness. For some, the need to always be right may be the result of permissive parenting, in which they always got whatever they wanted as a child. They never learned to compromise, accept the boundaries of others, or consider another person's needs and feelings. For others, the need to be right may come from a deep-seated place. Maybe when you were a child, no one valued your opinions or believed you when you said bad things were happening. As a result, you grew into an adult who is adamant about always being listened to and taken seriously. That makes sense. Even so, it's no way to live your life now if you want to have healthy relationships with others.

Try to soothe the young part of you in those moments: "Hey there, little (*your name here*), I know you want to be heard. I know it feels terrible when people don't listen to you and don't agree with you. It feels a lot like long ago when you were terrified and helpless and none of the adults around would step in to protect you. It's okay. I'm here now. Today is not like then, and this situation is different from that situation. Today we don't have to insist on always being right. We can compromise and see other points of view and still get our needs met."

Engaging in an inner dialogue to soothe that young, activated part of yourself can help get your wise, adult self back online so you can engage with others more constructively. Truthfully, the need to always be right is childish. If this is a problem for you, you need to look at the wounded child within you and heal that pain so you can show up in your life today as a healthy adult.

Heaven's Reward Fallacy

This is the final cognitive distortion. You can conceptualize heaven's reward fallacy as an expectation that you should always get a payoff for any sacrifice you make. "I worked every Saturday for six months to buy my teenager his first car. How dare he be disrespectful and stay out past curfew!" Well, because he is a teenager, and they are pretty much known for being careless, disrespectful, and selfish on occasion. It's less a reflection of his love and appreciation for you and more a reflection of his underdeveloped prefrontal cortex, which results in impulsiveness and poor judgment.

Sometimes you will sacrifice much, and the rewards will be handsome. Sometimes they won't. Just like the fallacy of fairness, if you always expect your sacrifices to be met with substantial rewards, you will end up being disappointed. Being prepared for things to not always work out perfectly in your favor is an excellent way to stay neutral about a variety of outcomes.

You aren't always going to get your just desserts in life, but that's not to say you shouldn't be hopeful. I want you to hope for happy results. Sometimes you're going to get just what you hoped for, and I want you to fully enjoy those moments. I also want you to be flexible and not be so fixated on specific outcomes that you can't be content when life gives you something other than what you wanted.

Do a Cost/Benefit Analysis

Changing your cognitive distortions and the unhealthy behaviors driven by those distortions might be the hardest part of posttraumatic growth. As we've already discussed, you developed those coping mechanisms because they worked, and they probably still work in some capacity. The problem is, they also have led to undesirable consequences. Self-growth requires self-awareness, and self-awareness can be painful.

An excellent way to begin shifting your cognitive distortions is to write out a good old-fashioned cost/benefit analysis. (You can use the template provided on the next few pages.) To begin, identify the cognitive distortions you engage in the most. You might want to order them from most to least problematic for you. Then for each distortion, write out the thoughts and behaviors you engage in that are driven by the distortion.

Next, consider the benefits of engaging in this behavior or way of thinking. There's a reason you developed a habit of thinking and behaving this way. What was it? How has it worked in meeting your needs? Get clear about how it has helped you or tricked you into thinking it was helpful. Examples might be "When I act helpless, others make decisions for me," "My aggressive behavior keeps people from challenging me," or "I don't risk getting hurt by others when I keep them at arm's length."

Finally, examine all the ways this thought or behavior hurts you. What is the cost of thinking or behaving this way? How has it already been harmful? How might it create more harm in the future if you don't shift gears? Seeing your challenges listed this way can be powerful and may provide the clarity you need to motivate real change. For example, you may not get hurt by others when you keep them at arm's length, but at what cost? You miss out on positive interactions and meaningful relationships. You rob yourself and others of joy, laughter, fun, intimacy, companionship, and belonging. You spend more time than necessary being alone and lonely, and you miss out on the human experience. That's a profound cost.

Once you identify, challenge, and intervene on your cognitive distortions, you are ready to step into posttraumatic growth and build that "life worth living" I spoke of earlier. It won't be a fairytale ending. It won't be the magic cure to get you to "love yourself." There will always be struggles, slipups, and suffering, because that's life. But there can also be peace, comfort, gentleness, and contentment too. You deserve that life. You really do.

Cognitive Distortions

Most Problematic to Least Problematic
1.
2.
3.
4.
5.

Distortion 1: ______________________________

Associated Thoughts and Behaviors:

____

____

____

____

____

____

Costs	Benefits

Distortion 2: ______________________________

Associated Thoughts and Behaviors:

____

____

____

____

____

____

Costs	Benefits

Distortion 3: ______________________________

Associated Thoughts and Behaviors:

____

____

____

____

____

____

Costs	Benefits

Distortion 4: ______________________________

Associated Thoughts and Behaviors:

____

____

____

____

____

____

Costs	Benefits

Distortion 5: ______________________________

Associated Thoughts and Behaviors:

____

____

____

____

____

____

Costs	Benefits

CHAPTER 12

Cultivate Peace, Happiness, and a Purposeful Life

Inner peace. What an elusive concept. What is it? Who has it? How do you get it and keep it in a world full of stress, responsibility, heartache, and tragedy? We can't all go to the mountains of Tibet, breathe in cold mountain air, and spend several hours a day in silent meditation. I have a lot of real-life issues that need my attention. I imagine you do too. Real life is often not conducive to living in a state of inner peace. So, how do we do it?

Well, sometimes we don't. First rule of inner peace: You aren't always going to feel peaceful. Sometimes you are going to be totally frazzled. You will still have moments of anger or frustration and the occasional complete meltdown. For me, part of being internally peaceful is accepting that those moments are going to come. When they do, they will feel awful, but I know I will get through them because eventually those terrible moments will pass and be replaced by better moments. I can count on that. Nothing I ever feel is permanent—no beautiful moment, no terrible situation, no feeling of bliss, no sense of agony. Every experience, sensation, and emotion I ever encounter is fleeting. It's the same for you too.

When you can accept that everything in life is temporary, it gives you the freedom to accept both the good and the bad without attaching yourself to it. Knowing that hard times are impermanent gives you the strength to endure them. Remembering that good times are temporary allows you to be fully present and appreciate them wholeheartedly.

The second rule of inner peace: You must practice real self-care—with *real* being the operative word. Since self-care has become a trendy topic on social media and many people have misconceptions about it, let's clear the air about what it is and isn't. Self-care is much more than how we spend our money to look good, feel good, prove we have value, or escape reality. Instead, self-care is about building a life of peace, contentment, and purpose. We all want to live a life we don't need to escape from so often.

You want to know what helps me? When I remind myself that all that media-driven noise is just a ploy to take my money and make other people rich off my insecurities. But I would be lying if I said knowing that in my head drowns out the noise entirely. So, I do my best. I seek what brings me genuine happiness. I ask myself, "What do I really value versus what media tells me to value?"

Ask yourself, "Am I surrounding myself with things I love, with things that make my life fulfilled and worth living?" If so, great. Each of us must create our own value system and live within it. I can't tell you what should or shouldn't make you happy. I can't tell you what you should or shouldn't value. That makes me no different from everyone else who is trying to sell you something. You get to decide for yourself what makes your life worth living. I only want to encourage you to find those answers from deep within yourself and not from a commercial, from self-comparison, or from the insults coming from your traumatized self.

It's also important for me to differentiate self-care from unhealthy comfort-seeking. Dr. Daniel Sumrok, director of the

Center for Addiction Science at the University of Tennessee Health Science Center College of Medicine, presented one of the most compelling theories on addiction I have ever read. He postulates that addiction is the result of ritualized, compulsive comfort-seeking.

Here's the thing about compulsive comfort-seeking: People who aren't living in a chronic state of pain don't need to seek comfort compulsively. But if I were living in a perpetual state of internal distress, I would look for any source of comfort to bring me relief, even if I knew it was temporary or destructive. No one can tolerate hurting all the time. Sometimes the desire for a moment of respite from pain can drive people to do things they know aren't good for them in the long run.

Dr. Sumrok attaches his theory to the ACE Study, highlighting correlations between the number of ACEs a person has and the level of chronic pain they live in, ultimately increasing their chances of becoming an addict. He advocates for addiction treatment with a focus on trauma therapy to reduce the chronic emotional pain of past trauma. Although he focuses primarily on substance use, I think all addictions apply. Whether you compulsively seek out food, relationships, sex, shopping, gambling, or drugs and alcohol, the motivating factor is the same: comforting the chronic pain.

We can easily apply this theory outside the context of addiction. I like to apply his concepts to all unhealthy, comfort-seeking behaviors. Examples include overworking, emotional eating, engaging in "retail therapy," excessively exercising, playing video games obsessively, binge-watching television, or engaging in risky, adrenaline-seeking behaviors. The more socially acceptable the behavior, the more likely we can get away with calling it "self-care."

Don't forget what I said earlier about self-care: The single most important act of self-care you can engage in is creating a life from which you don't feel the need to perpetually escape. That means if your drive to eat, go to happy hour, shop, work, exercise, have sex, play video games, or watch TV is internally demanding, it may not come from a healthy place.

The motivation to numb, distract, achieve, or just plain feel something might be more about comforting your chronic emotional pain than engaging in real self-care. True self-care is icing on the cake in a life that already feels largely satisfactory. If your "self-care" seems like a thing you need to do to get through the day or tolerate your life, your job, or your marriage, it's probably not real self-care. If your life sucks, no number of massages, great workouts, new purses, or martinis is going to fix it. Real self-care is about honoring your needs, engaging in what brings you contentment, and creating a satisfying life.

Cultivating Happiness

Let's transition from inner peace to happiness. Just as you won't always feel peaceful, no one can feel eternally happy either. We've already discussed how dangerous toxic positivity can be. But no matter how terrible your past, the human experience is filled with opportunities for connection, beauty, joy, and love. Sometimes you just need to make a concerted effort to find it.

To truly embrace the idea of happiness, you must first stop perpetuating your own suffering. This requires you to use your knowledge of radical acceptance. Remember, radical acceptance is the practice of accepting everything in your life as it is. People increase and prolong their suffering when they refuse to accept reality. You refuse to accept reality when you stay focused on what "should" be or what "should have" been.

For example, if I get a speeding ticket on the way to work, I can dwell all day on how I should have driven more slowly or how the officer should have been more understanding. However, obsessing about what should have been won't change the situation. I can accept I got a ticket on the way to work and acknowledge how much it sucks but not allow it to ruin my whole day.

I can choose radical acceptance and have a good (or neutral) day anyway. The result is the same in both cases because I have no control over the outcome. In one case, I suffer all day. In the other, I don't. I can let one shitty hour ruin an entire twenty-four hours, but I don't have to allow that. I have the power to focus on the present, noticing all the good and neutral experiences I have for the rest of the day. Remember, most of your life is spent in neutral moments. You just need to notice them. If I'm not actively dying and there isn't an imminent physical threat before me, I probably have the option to let go of an unhelpful thought and focus my attention on something more productive.

Let's talk about the attitude with which you walk through the world. Do you tend to encourage healthy, positive thoughts and intervene when you find yourself slipping into harmful, negative thoughts? Or do you tend to get stuck in negative thinking loops that perpetuate pain and suffering? Your answer will be a primary factor in how successful you are at maintaining self-neutrality, sustaining loving relationships with others, living a satisfactory life, and maintaining a peaceful heart.

As a note, people who tend to focus on the negative in life usually aren't miserable beings just looking for a reason to be unhappy. People who tend to focus on the positive in life aren't necessarily naive or in denial either. Both sets of people are living in and responding to their reality—and they are responding to the parts of their reality that get most of their attention.

It keeps coming back to that pesky negativity bias, which places emphasis on potential danger. Thank goodness for this cognitive function. It keeps us alive and safe. I am grateful for it. Unfortunately, it also prevents us from giving enough credit to all the good that happens around us. From an evolutionary perspective, that warm, fuzzy stuff just isn't as important. If we were still living in the wild, trying to avoid poison ivy and wolf attacks, we might not have time to focus on that glorious sunset or that peaceful walk we took among the trees.

Our brains just haven't caught up with the times. In our modern lives, we can have dozens of positive interactions with a spouse, for example, but as soon as they forget to pick up milk on the way home, it's easy to jump into "You always do this! You're so undependable! I do everything myself around here!" We must make intentional efforts to focus on all the parts of our reality, not just the immediate thoughts and emotions that come surging in when we are upset, anxious, disappointed, or uncertain.

Therefore, when you find yourself talking in extremes, like "I always" or "You never" statements, take a breath. That's your cue to pause, regroup, collect your wisest self, and revisit the situation from a grounded, balanced place.

The dysfunctional ways you respond to life today are probably a result of the same adaptive methods you developed to survive hardships earlier in your life. You might have lived a life in which you really couldn't count on others, where you had to do everything yourself. Your survival instincts were strong. You have every right to appreciate those adaptive parts of you.

However, it might not be true today that your spouse is undependable or that you must do everything around the house yourself. Those thoughts may reflect your old survival system kicking into gear, causing a reactive response. What helped you survive long ago may be unhelpful, unwarranted, and even destructive today. It's imperative to maintain self-awareness around how you respond to stressors in your life now. You can and should express gratitude to the survivor parts of you, but if they interfere with your ability to be your best self today, it's time to throw those parts a retirement party and let them go.

Looking from the Outside In

In my personal healing journey, I often thought about my life as a movie in which I was the main character. I had a troubled past and many struggles because of that past. I was the protagonist, which meant I was the good guy, the hero, the one to root for throughout the story. This helped me step out of myself and my own self-criticism and see things from an outside perspective, which made it easier for me to stay on my own team, so to speak.

Essentially, I used the concept of the hero's journey to encourage myself to keep moving through the healing process. If you aren't already familiar with it, the hero's journey is a template used by writers when creating the vision for a plot. The short version is: The hero gets some sort of call to adventure, follows the call, faces obstacles (villains, perhaps), must make painful decisions, gets a little help from other travelers along the way, ultimately experiences victory, and returns home forever transformed by the experience.

You are the hero in the story of your life. You were born into this world and called to adventure. What your adventure is, I cannot say. Perhaps you were called to create art or music; be a healer, teacher, or leader; or roam the world as a perpetual student and philosopher. Maybe your dreams involve finding a partner, creating a peaceful home, and raising a loving family. Whatever your calling, it's yours to discover and cultivate.

As I write this book at forty-six years old, I realize I have received many calls to adventure. I'm not sure any of them have been my "one true purpose." My life has been a kaleidoscope of experiences and callings that all seemed meaningful at the time. I think it's okay to have various missions and many adventures that change over time as you do. If you're searching for meaning in your life and you aren't sure what your "great calling" is, don't sweat it. Maybe you'll figure it out. Perhaps you'll just grow and keep evolving into better versions of yourself and find an adventure in each passing chapter of your life. That has felt productive and satisfying to me over the years, at least.

But back to *your* hero's journey. It has led you here, to a book about how to heal your trauma, stop hating yourself, and find peace in your life. That in and of itself says you have been called to an adventure of self-growth. That's awesome. So far, you have delved into your deep past to face down the monsters that created your insecurities and self-doubt. Your "villains" may have been specific people from your past but also may have been unavoidable adverse childhood experiences. Your hang-ups may have come from well-meaning but hurtful parenting techniques or from bullying by other kids going through their own hardships. You may have lived in the shadow of a superstar sibling or had a sick parent. Maybe you grew up in an impoverished, dangerous community with an underfunded school and limited resources to create a better life.

Perhaps you had to reconcile how you were different from those around you: a dark-skinned person living in a light-skinned community, a gay person living in a straight community, or a person with a disability living in a physically unaccommodating community. As we've already discussed, you don't have to be the victim of severe child abuse to become an adult with massive insecurities and an inability to love yourself. Whatever your challenges entailed, they are valid. Their impact has been real. You get to unapologetically own your truth. If you made it from a challenging childhood into adulthood, you're a survivor in one way or another.

Many of you reading this are abuse survivors, and for those who resonate with that, I want to give you this message: Your abusers, whomever they were or are, tried to break you. But you are here, connected with these words at this moment, which means they failed. You survived, and now you have been called to build a victorious life for yourself. Though they tried to break you, they unleashed the warrior within you. You are on your hero's journey, and you are in the phase of obstacles and challenges. Like the phoenix, you will rise. I know this because I rose out of my own ashes and because I have worked with so many who rose out of theirs.

You are powerful. It is the power within you that allowed you to survive your darkest hours. It's the same power that brought you to this moment of reckoning. You are fighting for yourself right now, which makes you a real hero. You have not always been in a position of power in your life. Others have had control over you, for a variety of reasons. That time is over. It's time to take your power back.

Incorporating Curiosity

People who remain self-neutral are neither jealous nor toxically competitive. They don't hope others will fail so they can feel better about themselves. They don't look for reasons to condemn the looks or behaviors of others so they can feel "better than."

People who are healing know there is enough room for all of us to be fulfilled in life. There is enough love and joy in the world for all of us to have a slice. I don't need to cut anyone down, minimize anyone's accomplishments, or downplay another person's greatness to feel okay about myself.

In Brené Brown's book *Daring Greatly*, she explains how people are most judgmental when they feel inadequate. She discusses the way mothers criticize other moms for their parenting, not because they believe they are perfect mothers themselves, but because they know they aren't. When a mother feels insecure about her parenting, she may feel compelled to judge the actions of other moms to feel "good enough" by being "better than" her. If I stay grounded and neutral about myself, I can believe I am a "good enough" mom (even though I am a totally imperfect mom). This belief allows me to not care if you breastfeed or bottle-feed, use cloth or disposable diapers, homeschool or public-school your kids, and so on. I don't need to put myself above other women to feel adequate. I do me. You do you. I'm rooting for us both.

I listened to a psychiatrist give a keynote speech once in which he shared how he processes his own judgment. He said when he realizes he is being critical toward himself or another person, he pauses and notices his internal process with curiosity. When a person is engaging in a judgmental thought, they will often do one of two things with it. They may choose to accept the idea as truth and open the floodgates for more judgment. They might say something like: "Look at that woman in those nasty sweatpants. Did she even brush her hair before she left the house? I would never let myself go out like that." Or they may immediately be critical of themselves for having the judgmental thought: "Ugh, I am such a jerk! This lady is just living her life! Why do I have an ugly thing to say about everyone? I can't stand myself sometimes."

Taking a third approach, curiosity, allows you to do something different. You might say to yourself, "That's interesting. I'm having a judgmental thought about this person. I wonder what that says about how I feel about me right now?" This allows you to move from judgment to a neutral state of noticing.

We can engage in curiosity when we are critical toward ourselves too. Let's say I notice myself having the thought "I can't believe I said that! I'm such an idiot!" I have a few options: I can accept the thought as truth: "That was idiotic. Everyone must think I am a complete moron. I'm never going to show my face here again!" I can beat myself up for it: "Dammit, Heidi! Stop talking to yourself like that, you miserable cow!" Or I can embrace the thought without judgment and with curiosity: "Well, that's interesting. I'm being unreasonably hard on myself right now. I wonder what is going on with me. I must be feeling vulnerable and insecure in this moment."

This third option allows me the opportunity to offer compassion for my insecurity, the way I would for a friend experiencing self-doubt and anxiety. It lets me approach myself with words like "Okay, Heidi, it's not a big deal. It wasn't the most eloquent thing I've ever said, but it's unlikely anyone else thought much of it. Even if they did, I can always clarify later and make the situation right. I'm being brave by putting myself out there, and I am doing it imperfectly, just like everyone else. It's okay. I'm okay." In this last scenario, I practice having both compassion and kindness for myself, and I accept the reality of the situation without minimizing or catastrophizing it. This allows me to stay grounded and balanced and perceive myself in a neutral way.

A Life Worth Living

Are you ready to create a life worth living? You've probably heard the old saying, "People who are happy don't have the best of everything, they just make the best of everything." There is a lot of truth to that. Some of the happiest people I have encountered have relatively little in the way of material possessions. They aren't rich or powerful, and they aren't always beautiful or influential. They certainly aren't perfect. They have encountered significant challenges: illness, physical disability, children with special needs, family members with addiction, career setbacks, financial hardships, horrible injustices, and yes, terrible traumas. But their lives are still rich with love, purpose, passion, joy, and meaningful relationships. They have defined what they value most. They are clear about what is important to them and what is just filler.

Let's be real. None of us have the answer. There are some universal truths, but most of us are just fumbling around, doing our best, trying to learn from our experiences and lead the best lives we can. I've witnessed scores of people move out of dis-ease and into happiness and self-neutrality, and I've done it myself. In the next section, I'll share with you what I've seen work in my own practice and my own life, in hopes that it can be helpful for you too.

Define Your Values

First, I think it is imperative to define your values. What matters to you most? What elements of life are a requirement for you to feel fulfilled? I suggest you make a values list. Think about what is underneath each value. For example, if you put "become a mother" as a value, what is it about parenthood that's so important to you? Be clear about it. That way, if you don't become a mother, you open up the possibility of it not becoming a source of despair. Perhaps the value underneath your desire to be a parent is that you want to love and be loved, or you want your presence, guidance, and wisdom to be meaningful to others. Maybe you value mentorship and want to help others achieve their dreams. Parenthood is a natural source for integrating these values into your life, but it isn't the only way.

Once you have whittled down to the purest elements of each value on your list, ask yourself, "What are all the ways I can incorporate this value into my life? How can I start incorporating these elements right now?" Don't wait until after you have a college degree, get that dream job, get married, have a specific dollar amount in your bank account, or overcome whatever other limitations you put on yourself to keep that "if/when" fallacy thriving in your head.

Do you value travel and adventure? Great! Open yourself up to the possibilities there. Take a weekend road trip. Go camping. Try geocaching. Find out where all the best views or lakes are in your state and go see them. Drive to the nearest beach and make yourself a sandcastle. Check out some quirky mom-and-pop restaurants in your area owned by people from countries you would like to visit. You don't have to wait until you have the time and money for that bucket-list trip to Europe. Start enjoying and exploring the world around you now.

Do you value learning? Take a class at a community college. Find some great podcasts or books on subjects interesting to you. Check out museums in your area. Make a commitment to yourself to master something you've always wanted to learn. Pick up an instrument or a foreign language. Learn to cook, paint, build furniture, or repurpose old household items. You don't have to get a college degree to learn. You don't have to dedicate twenty hours a week to a learning endeavor. You can invest two hours a week. You can commit to fifteen minutes a day. Do whatever makes sense in your life. Don't avoid doing something that would enrich your life now just because you tell yourself you don't have time to do it perfectly.

Do you value meaningful relationships? Wonderful! Take stock of the relationships you have. Are they fulfilling? Fun? Do they make you feel good about yourself? Do you feel honored, valued, and cared about? If not, decide what you can control. Try to improve relationships you want to salvage by setting boundaries and asking for your needs to be met. Give yourself permission to let go of relationships that are harmful. Even if you've already invested considerable time and energy into them, even if they are blood relations, you are never obligated to engage with people who make you feel like crap.

Find your people. Join a meetup group or a book club, find a place of worship that jibes with your soul, or join a community group on Facebook. Can't find the kind of group you're looking for? Start it! Take a class at your local community center. Offer to teach a class at your local community center. Audition at your local community theater or offer to be a part of the production team. Volunteer at a local nonprofit that does something you feel passionate about. You can cuddle sick babies, take shelter dogs on walks, make food boxes for hungry families, teach women escaping domestic violence how to put a résumé together, or be a mentor to an at-risk youth.

Whatever your strengths or interests are, there is an organization that would love to have you. Your like-minded people are out there. You may have to work a little to find them. Don't let that stop you from seeking out the people who will fill your heart with love, purpose, and joy.

Identify Accountability Partners

These should be friends or family members you trust with the most intimate details of your life. People with whom you feel safe saying, "Hey, I'm working on taking better care of myself, being self-compassionate, and making healthier choices. I want to tell you what I'm working on and ask you to check in with me and help me stay accountable." These should be people who don't have a personal agenda with you. People who don't have a vested interest in your choices or behavior make the best accountability partners.

Ideally, you will have at least three people in your life who can serve this purpose. Of course, you should offer to do the same for them, opening the door to a meaningful, emotionally intimate relationship in which you are able to mutually share the more vulnerable parts of yourselves safely. Look for and be the kind of accountability partner who is willing to offer empathy and support, who is ready to call out BS when you see it, and who will hold someone's feet to the fire from a place of love and good intention.

I don't want my accountability partners to always agree with me or tell me I'm right. My truest friends call me out. They tell me when I'm being too rigid or unkind, or when I'm overreacting. I do the same for them because we love each other and want each of us to be our happiest, healthiest, best selves. Sometimes you need someone who loves you enough to give you a dose of reality to set you straight.

Indulge in the Scandinavian Practice of Hygge

I'm the daughter of a Norwegian immigrant, and one of my favorite Scandinavian traditions is the practice of *hygge* (pronounced hue-gah). This is generally a winter practice, and the term can be roughly translated as "coziness." When you've done everything you know to do and nothing is working, decide to call it a day. Go home. Order food delivery. Turn on a movie. Cuddle under your blankets, sip a cup of cocoa, pile all your fluffiest pillows around you, light some candles, draw a bath—you get the picture.

Sometimes everything is shit. It's okay to acknowledge it, initiate a reset, and try again tomorrow.

Repeat Self-Neutral Affirmations

Last, I want to encourage you to go back to those self-neutral affirmations we talked about earlier in this book. Sometimes the only affirmations you can make are the ones that keep you from making a bad situation worse. Troubling times are a part of life for everyone. When you don't have any better options, you can use the skills you've gained from this book to make self-neutral statements like:

- This completely sucks, but I will survive it.
- I made a mistake, and I'll fix it later when I'm in a better mindset.
- I don't know what I'm doing, but I will figure it out eventually.
- That wasn't a great choice, but I understand why I chose it in the moment. I was doing my best, but I can do better next time.
- Everybody fails sometimes. I will try again when I'm ready.
- It's okay to hate this and wish things were different. It can't be different right now, so I just need to tolerate it the best I can until things get better.
- The reality is, this is all I can handle at the moment, and that will have to do for now.

Radical acceptance, self-acceptance, and (hopefully) a little patience and self-kindness will be the safety net you'll fall into time and again to save yourself from plummeting into that pit of self-hatred when times get tough. You always have tomorrow to get clear on your posttraumatic goals again, come back to your values and priorities, and recommit to your personal mission. When you don't have it in you, just let that be okay. When you are ready, your internal and external resources will be there to get you back on track.

Afterword: Life Beyond Trauma

I wrote this book in the hopes that you will begin to see that you are not doomed to a miserable life of self-hatred, trapped by the ghosts of your complex trauma. Your trauma healing process is a unique path you will carve out for yourself. You don't have to subscribe to anyone else's theories or road maps.

I hope you will continue to practice self-neutrality as an alternative to self-loathing, self-acceptance as an alternative to trauma repetition, and self-compassion as an alternative to hateful self-talk. As I've discussed, none of these things will come naturally or easily, but with dedication and consistency, they are all very real options for the rest of your life. Before I leave you, let's review the major concepts we've covered throughout this book.

The Power of Your Internal Voice

We all have an internal voice, which is a composite of all the voices we have heard throughout our lives. For complex trauma survivors, that voice can be cruel and hateful.

- What kind of statements do you make to yourself, about yourself?
- What are the negative core beliefs you hold about yourself that drive your critical self-talk?

This is the voice of your trauma. Actively reject that voice and make intentional efforts to engage in neutral self-talk based on your newfound knowledge of the neuroscience of trauma.

Unpack Your Personal Trauma History

Find an amazing trauma therapist. Create a trauma inventory, like the trauma egg. Honor the younger versions of yourself whose pain still lives inside you. Your self-defeating voice emerged to protect you from painful experiences, but today it is simply the voice of fear.

Many people fear that acknowledging their pain will break them—that they will be trapped in a sadness they won't be able to escape. You need to fight past that fear. You can feel your pain and move through to the other side of it. Acknowledging your hurt will not trap you in it. If you broke your arm, would you ignore the pain, hoping it will just go away if you don't think about it? Of course not. You would listen to your body, acknowledge the reality of your wound, and seek medical help. You would do what you needed to do, even if it was uncomfortable, so you could heal properly and move on. You need to treat your trauma in this thoughtful way.

Cultivate Self-Neutrality

This is an intentional practice that requires repetition. You must begin treating yourself with compassion, care, and respect. You have always deserved to treat yourself this way. Your painful early life experiences and the self-defeating thoughts that emerged because of them have tricked you into believing you aren't worthy of self-kindness or understanding. Be mindful. Use neuroplasticity to your advantage. Engage in daily exercises to foster a state of self-neutrality. Do it no matter how much you hate it in the beginning and despite how certain you are it won't work. The research says it works. People like you are healing. You are not the exception to humanity. Remain consistent and trust the process.

Consume Content Carefully

Social media can be an amazing place to learn and connect with people to whom you can relate. Just remember there is a lot of terrible information out there, and comparing your healing journey to anyone else's has the potential to make you feel unnecessarily worse. Quit gaslighting yourself and stop repeating ideas that make you feel worse about yourself. Get out of your head and use the power of your mind to control your thoughts. Your mind is powerful. What you attend to will become your reality.

Recognize Your Power

You aren't a helpless child anymore. You have choices. You don't get to choose everything, but you have some power of choice in nearly every situation you ever find yourself in. Choose to react differently. Choose to look at the situation from a different perspective. Choose to speak differently to yourself about what happens. It's not about ignoring reality. It's about acknowledging and accepting all parts of reality, not just the negative parts.

You reviewed the most common types of cognitive distortions and learned tools for reframing these faulty ways of thinking. Look at the ways you are defensive, offensive, passive-aggressive, stubborn, selfish, manipulative, and victim-posturing. Only when you are willing to face the underbelly of your own dysfunction can you shift the way you think and behave in meaningful ways. Decide who you want to be in your posttraumatic growth. Set challenging but doable goals and create a realistic plan to meet those goals.

Cultivate a Life Worth Living

It's time to replace unhealthy behaviors with healthier, more adaptive ones. Stop being afraid of enjoying life and give yourself permission to embrace all the good and neutral parts of life without hyper-focusing on the bad parts. You can develop inner peace by using skills such as radical acceptance, self-compassion, mindfulness, and self-acceptance. Being nonjudgmental toward yourself and others is an essential component of this step. Accept what you can and cannot control, and learn to let go in situations involving the latter. Finally, cultivate a self-care practice. When everything is falling apart, know when to call it a day and go into your self-care space until you're ready to face the world again.

Foster a Life of Purpose

Define your values and create a life built around those values. Start doing things that make you happy, feed your soul, and allow you to be a helper for others. Hold yourself accountable and ask the people you trust to hold you accountable. Your trauma was not your fault, but recovery is your responsibility. You can't wait for a better life to find you. You need to build it for yourself. You are the master of your destiny and the author of the rest of your life's story.

So, there you have it, an alternative to letting complex trauma ruin the rest of your life. You have everything you need inside you to overcome your past, be your healthiest self, and live a satisfying life in which you are no longer plagued by self-loathing. I may not know you, but I believe in you. I believe in your goodness, your worth, your strength, and your capability. I believe in you because, like me, you are a survivor. You have come this far, and you have a hunger to be better than you are today. You long for a different kind of life. That hunger, that longing, your survival thus far—they all tell me you are worthy and capable. You wouldn't have read this book in its entirety if you didn't know somewhere inside you that it's true.

All journeys eventually reach their end, and we have arrived at the point where you are ready to continue traveling toward trauma healing and self-neutrality without me. Though we part ways here, I hope you keep my words of encouragement and resiliency in your heart as you continue onward. I honor you now as you step out of survival mode and into a life worth living. Your human experience matters. You are supposed to be here. You are meant to enjoy being alive. We've all heard the saying "It gets better." This is it. This is where it gets better. The rest is up to you.

References

Introduction

***The Path to Self-Love & World Domination* is a great book for people with a history of trauma who believe they can love themselves and who want to find a path to self-love by resolving their unhealed wounds:** Green, H. (2020). *The path to self-love & world domination: Break free from self-limiting beliefs and embrace your power.* Health Communications.

Chapter 2

Dr. Temple Grandin discusses how distress impedes learning in animals, just as it does in humans: Grandin, T. (2010). *Animals make us human.* Mariner Books.

Chapter 3

There was a groundbreaking research project conducted in Southern California through the Centers for Disease Control and Prevention (CDC) and Kaiser Permanente in the late 1990s: Felitti, V. J., Anda, R. F., Nordenberg, D., Williamson, D. F., Spitz, A. M., Edwards, V., & Marks, J. S. (1998). Relationship of childhood abuse and household dysfunction to many of the leading causes of death in adults: The Adverse Childhood Experiences (ACE) Study. *American Journal of Preventive Medicine, 14*(4), 245–258. https://doi.org/10.1016/S0749-3797(98)00017-8

Researchers developed a corresponding scale to measure positive childhood experiences, called the Benevolent Childhood Experiences (BCEs) Scale: Narayan, A. J., Rivera, L. M., Bernstein, R. E., Harris, W. W., & Lieberman, A. F. (2018). Positive childhood experiences predict less psychopathology and stress in pregnant women with childhood adversity: A pilot study of the Benevolent Childhood Experiences (BCEs) scale. *Child Abuse and Neglect, 78*, 19–30. https://doi.org/10.1016/j.chiabu.2017.09.022

Chapter 4

There are four components of DBT: Linehan, M. (2014). *DBT skills training manual* (2nd ed.). Guilford Press.

People who talked to themselves like a good friend for seven days in a row lowered their depression levels for three months and raised their happiness levels for six months: Shapira, L. B., & Mongrain, M. (2010).

The benefits of self-compassion and optimism exercises for individuals vulnerable to depression. *The Journal of Positive Psychology, 5*(5), 377–389. https://doi.org/10.1080/17439760.2010.516763

Meditators had significantly less pain after eight weeks: Carson, J. W., Keefe, F. J., Lynch, T. R., Carson, K. M., Goli, V., Fras, A. M., & Thorp, S. R. (2005). Loving-kindness meditation for chronic low back pain: Results from a pilot trial. *Journal of Holistic Nursing, 23*(3), 287–304. https://doi.org/10.1177/0898010105277651

Another study out of Boston College examined people with chronic back pain: Arnstein, P., Vidal, M., Wells-Federman, C., Morgan, B., & Caudill, M. (2002). From chronic pain patient to peer: Benefits and risks of volunteering. *Pain Management Nursing, 3*(3), 94–103. https://doi.org/10.1053/jpmn.2002.126069

In his book *I Heart Me*, Dr. David Hamilton offers four additional self-compassion strategies: Hamilton, D. (2015). *I heart me: The science of self-love.* Hay House.

Chapter 6

Self-compassion is an act of loving and accepting yourself despite your failures **and weaknesses:** Neff, K. (2015). *Self-compassion: The proven power of being kind to yourself.* William Morrow Paperbacks.

Chapter 7

***Men Are from Mars, Women Are from Venus*, which has been criticized for oversimplifying complex human dynamics and romantic relationships:** Gray, J. (1992). *Men are from Mars, women are from Venus.* HarperCollins.

Chapter 8

Dr. Aaron Beck, widely recognized as the father of cognitive therapy: Beck, A. (1979). *Cognitive therapy and the emotional disorders: A major exploration of an influential approach to the understanding and treatment of mental illness.* Penguin.

Chapter 9

The practice of learned optimism requires you to accept that emotional well-being can be intentionally cultivated: Seligman, M. E. P. (2006). *Learned optimism: How to change your mind and your life.* Vintage.

Her trauma treatment model, known as the Murray Method®, helps clients explore their past and make connections between their early life experiences

and their current day struggles: Murray, M. (2012). *The Murray Method: The internationally acclaimed approach to becoming a health balanced person.* Vivo Publications.

Chapter 10

Therapists have a few traits they look for in the beginning of treatment, one of which is a client's window of tolerance: Siegel, D. J. (1999). *The developing mind: Toward a neurobiology of interpersonal experience.* Guilford Press.

The practice of *positive psychology*, a term first coined by Dr. Martin Seligman: Seligman, M. E. P. (1999). The president's address. *American Psychologist, 54*(8), 559–562.

Author Yehuda Berg once wrote: Berg, Y. [@yehudaberg]. (2013, June 17). *If you look for the bad, you will find it. If you look for the good, you will find it* [Post]. X. https://x.com/yehudaberg/status/346825773245669376

London cab drivers have thick neural layers in the hippocampus: Maguire, E. A., Woollett, K., & Spiers, H. J. (2006). London taxi drivers and bus drivers: A structural MRI and neuropsychological analysis. *Hippocampus, 16*(12), 1091–1101. https://doi.org/10.1002/hipo.20233

Mindfulness meditators have increased gray matter: Hanson, R. (2013). *Hardwiring happiness: The new brain science of contentment, calm, and confidence.* Harmony Books.

Chapter 11

Dr. Beck identified fifteen primary cognitive distortions that require awareness and intervention: Beck, A. (1979). *Cognitive therapy and the emotional disorders: A major exploration of an influential approach to the understanding and treatment of mental illness.* Penguin.

Chapter 12

One of the most compelling theories on addiction I have ever read: Stevens, J. E. (2017, May 2). *Addiction doc says: It's not the drugs. It's the ACEs… Adverse childhood experiences.* Aces Too High News. https://acestoohigh.com/2017/05/02/addiction-doc-says-stop-chasing-the-drug-focus-on-aces-people-can-recover/

People are most judgmental when they feel inadequate: Brown, B. (2015). *Daring greatly: How the courage to be vulnerable transforms the way we live, love, parent, and lead.* Avery.

Acknowledgments

My heart is full of gratitude for the mentors and colleagues who have inspired my personal and professional growth. Thank you to the many talented therapists who helped me heal my personal trauma. Thank you to Dr. John Toma and Dr. Marcus Earle, cherished mentors who took me under their wings and taught me how childhood trauma impacts the rest of our lives. Thank you to the fellow psychologists and therapists who have worked alongside me throughout my career. You have been such wonderful friends and teachers.

To my many clients over the years, please know how much our time together means to me. Thank you for trusting me with your stories, which have touched my soul forever. Walking with you on your journey to healing has been one of the greatest honors of my life.

Finally, to Kate Sample, Roseanne Cheng, Jenessa Jackson, and the team at PESI Publishing, many thanks for making books about mental health healing available to the public. Thank you for believing in my message and trusting me to deliver it. I am so grateful for all the hard work and dedication you put into bringing my book to life.

About the Author

Heidi Green, PsyD, is a licensed clinical psychologist and trauma therapist who provides telehealth to clients across the United States through her private practice. Prior to this book, she authored *The Path to Self-Love & World Domination*. Dr. Green maintains an active social media presence on Instagram (@drheidigreen), where she provides education and inspiration on a range of mental health topics. She is also a workshop facilitator who provides certification training in trauma therapy to mental health professionals through PESI. Dr. Green is an experienced keynote speaker and enjoys speaking to groups interested in the effects of complex trauma. If you would like to learn more about how to work with Dr. Green, please visit her website: drheidigreen.com.